PURPOSE AND POWER
IN RETIREMENT

PURPOSE
and POWER
IN RETIREMENT

new opportunities
for meaning and significance

HAROLD G. KOENIG, M.D.

TEMPLETON FOUNDATION PRESS
PHILADELPHIA AND LONDON

Templeton Foundation Press
Five Radnor Corporate Center. Suite 120
100 Matsonford Road
Radnor, Pennsylvania 19087

Library of Congress Cataloging-in-Publication Data
Koenig, Harold George.
  Purpose and power in retirement : new opportunities for meaning
and significance / Harold G. Koenig.
    p. cm.
Includes bibliographical references and index.
  ISBN 1-932031-33-2 (pbk : alk. paper)
  1. Retirement. 2. Retirees—Life skills guides. 3. Self-actualization
(Psychology) I. Title.
  HQ1062 .K625 2002
  646.7'9—dc21
                                        2002003984

Printed in the United States of America by Hamilton Printing Company
Designed and typeset in Goudy by Gopa & Ted2

www. templetonpress.org

03 04 05 06 07 08   10 9 8 7 6 5 4 3 2 1

To my son Jordan Taylor Koenig,
a growing young man with purpose

❧ Contents

❧ Foreword

D<small>R. K</small>OENIG is a remarkable and intelligent doctor and professor of medicine who specializes in trying to help the rapidly growing number of people who are moving from middle age into their later years, who are either retired or who are considering retirement. This helpful book raises the question of whether idleness leads to the production of goods and discoveries and happiness, or whether it produces the opposite. If you have observed large numbers of people over age sixty-five, do you find that those who are idle are healthier and more satisfied, or do you find that they tend to decline more rapidly in body and mind, as well as in happiness and self-esteem?

Furthermore, is it sensible to think that the vast cosmos was created for the purpose of producing happiness for a single species on one little planet? Humans have not yet discovered any other species anywhere with the ability to plan for progress and for the expansion of information. Does this raise the question of whether we may have been created to serve as helpers in the acceleration of divine creativity?

Do these observations imply that creativity can bring more benefits and more happiness than can idleness? Before the twentieth century, it was customary all over the world for people to work as long as they were able. It was rare for a person to change from being a producer to being a parasite on a nation's resources. The idea that a nation or an employer should provide a pension was almost unknown.

Recently, a major nation established a police force to prevent any person from holding employment after age fifty-five and to prevent any person from being employed over thirty-five hours weekly. What do you think will happen to the productivity of that nation? Will the younger and more industrious people want to leave? Instead of forcing idleness, would it not be more helpful to give incentives for more work, for inventions, and for entrepreneurship?

In America, when Franklin Roosevelt was president, the first national Social Security system was adopted; it set the retirement age at sixty-five. At the time sixty-five was the average life expectancy; therefore, only about half the people would live to collect Social Security. The total cost of the program was reasonable. The increasing burden of paying for Social Security today could have been avoided if the retirement age had been made adjustable for changes in average life expectancy. Today such a change would not likely gain a majority of votes in Congress. However, quite possibly a majority of votes would favor a proposal to place no income tax on the earnings of people who work beyond age sixty-five. That would be a blessing not only for individuals but also for the national economy.

Recently, more Americans have begun to advocate that after age sixty-five a person should become active as a volunteer for a church or a charity. Already America leads the world in volunteering and millions of people are productive and happier because they have volunteered. However, when you think about it, would it not also be wise to begin helping teenagers to plan their careers so that they could be beneficial and productive until they are disabled? In many careers, people can remain productive until age seventy-five or eighty-five.

Of course, there are some careers where it would be necessary to plan ahead for a different career. For example, a great surgeon whose hands begin to tremble might have prepared in advance to be a teacher, lecturer, or researcher. Similarly, some of us would prefer not to fly in an airplane whose pilot was over seventy-five; but in this case as well, through conscious planning a pilot could prepare him or herself for a later career. In addition, rather than planning to live on government handouts, perhaps most young people could be taught to create a diversified investment plan for unexpected emergencies. While planning for a beneficial and happy career after age sixty-five, most people could also begin at age twenty-five to build a diversified portfolio of assets, which would enable them to finance new enterprises and charities as long as they live.

I hope that many schools and universities and churches and employers will want to provide encouragement and education so that almost everyone will make a wise plan for later life. Textbooks can reveal the glorious lives of old benefactors. At age eighty-nine I am busier than ever, more enthusiastic and joyful than ever, because I am working on dozens of programs to help humanity gain more spiritual wealth. If you want such joy and enthusiasm too, then continue reading.

Sir John Templeton

PURPOSE AND POWER
IN RETIREMENT

❧ Introduction

"Many persons have a wrong idea of what constitutes true happiness. It is not attained through self-gratification but through fidelity to a worthy purpose." —Helen Keller

S ITTING IN MY BACKYARD one Saturday morning, I was deep in thought. It was a couple of days after my fiftieth birthday. I had just received a letter in the mail from the American Association of Retired Persons. It both shocked me and ticked me off. But it started me thinking. What will I do with my time when I retire? That decision will affect the quality of the rest of my life. I'd really like to put the decision off for a while. If I wait, though, inaction now will also have an impact on my future. I've heard that when people retire, their time quickly fills up with activities. I'm afraid that the meaning of my final years could be lost—a huge opportunity missed or at least not fully realized.

Since I'm only going to live once and this is my last chance, I don't want to miss the real purpose of why I'm here—especially why I'm here in this place and at this time. I believe my life has a purpose and that my Christian faith has something to do with it. I don't believe that I am simply the result of random forces or impersonal chance in a merciless universe intent on snuffing me out and returning me to the atoms and molecules from whence I came. If there is a purpose to my life, then I'm determined not to allow anything to stand in the way of that purpose—especially my lack of knowledge of options and con-sequences. I want to be prepared so that when I leave my job in a few years, I will know where I'm headed in the next phase of my life. After all, that phase may last another twenty-five or thirty years. I'm going to start my planning early.

I wonder if my friends and colleagues are also thinking about this issue. What will they do when they retire? This isn't some-thing you typically talk about during work or social conversa-tions, but it must be on their minds, especially if they are anywhere between the ages of fifty and sixty. I suspect that after they leave the workplace, many will understandably choose a life of leisure, self-enjoyment, and recreation within the limits of their health and finances. I certainly don't blame them. They have worked hard for many years, sacrificing time and pleasure to support their families and perhaps to accumulate a little nest egg to kick back on. It certainly seems like that's what everybody is doing. Maybe I should do that, too.

I wish I could simply plan to do that and stop worrying about it. But there is that persistent, nagging thought: *I want more out of life.* I want to continue to make a difference in the world. As Kay Whitmore said, "Making a difference is not easy. But the price of indifference is too great not to try." Are there any bet-ter options than simply stepping aside and focusing on leisure, trying to stay busy to keep from getting bored?

I know that I'm not alone with these struggles. Consider the following people:

♦ John had his fifty-fifth birthday last month. He has been thinking a lot lately about what he will do when he leaves the job he's been at for the past thirty years. Should he seek early retirement in a couple of years or go the dis-tance to age sixty-five? That time seems to be approaching faster and faster, much faster than he ever dreamed. John enjoys his work, which has given him much personal fulfillment. Most of his friends are also from his job. Work structures his entire week. How will he spend his time when he doesn't have to be at the office every morning?

• Josie, age sixty-seven, is widowed and living by herself in an apartment. Her arthritis has limited her activities over the past few years. She has two children with families who live nearby, but they are consumed with their own jobs and kids and are not able to include her as often as she would like them to. She spends a lot of time at home, worrying about her health, watching television, and feeling lonely.

• Jim just turned sixty-six. He retired last year from a position in a lumber company where he had operated heavy machinery for nearly four decades. Jim worked hard physically for many years, taking orders from his supervisors and dutifully carrying them out. Despite being a devoted employee, he never really liked the work and often dreamed of starting his own business and being his own boss some day. But it never happened. Through the years, he consoled himself with the thought that if he worked hard and handled his money right, he would eventually be able to leave his job and enjoy some fun and travel. During the past year Jim and his wife traveled around the United States and even took a trip to Europe for two weeks. For the last several months, however, he has begun to grow bored, wondering if this is all there is to life.

• Joan has been employed at the telephone company for the past twenty-five years. Because of downsizing and budget cuts, she recently learned that her boss wants her to retire in six months when she reaches age sixty. All of her children are raised and out of the house, and her husband is still busy managing his business. She wonders what she will do after she leaves her job.

What about you? Have you been thinking about retirement lately, even though it's still a long way off? Or is it just around the corner? Are you retired and wondering how to make this time in your life more worthwhile and meaningful? Do you want a vision for the last third of your life that will give you a reason to get up in the morning and be excited about the day ahead? Do you want these last precious years to be fulfilling and satisfying? Do you want, as I do, to still make a difference in the world around you? Do you want direction and purpose in your life, even when you become sick, lose loved ones, or encounter the many other changes that aging is likely to bring? If your answer to any of these questions is yes, then this book was written for you.

If you're in that first category of people starting to think seriously about retirement, I'll bet you're among the first wave of 80 million baby boomers preparing themselves to leave work about five to ten years down the road. In the year 2011, this huge group of now late middle-aged Americans will start turning sixty-five. If you have already retired, then you are probably among the 30 million persons over age sixty-five that have left full-time work either because they chose to or because they were forced out by employers or by poor health. Regardless of where you are in these categories, there are opportunities to achieve purpose and power, both now and in the years ahead.

Before we begin, however, I'd like to explain what the words in the title of this book mean. I'll address them in reverse order: retirement, power, and purpose. Conceptions of retirement vary widely. Many see it as a time to finally start having some leisure and fun without the burden of ever having to go to work or take orders from someone else again; as a time to step aside and let the younger people take over all the responsibilities and challenges of being in the work force; or as a time to focus on their own needs for a change, rather than on the demands of others.

In an economic sense, retirement is simply the departure from paid labor.[1] This economic definition, however, is not very satisfying or descriptive. I like this one better: "Retirement is the last one-third of life that no longer has the restrictions of the first two-thirds." The first one-third of life is spent growing up, obtaining an education, and perhaps meeting a spouse and having children. The middle third of life is spent raising one's children and advancing in one's job or profession. Once the children are raised and leave the house and formal work life has ended, the final one-third of life begins—retirement—the last stage, the final lap, a time of *unprecedented new opportunities*.

Power is the second word in the title that needs attention. Webster's dictionary defines power as "the ability to do, act or produce." Power is typically associated with youth, physical speed, strength, independence, and mental agility. It can also be associated with maturity and influence, as a king may have power over subjects in his kingdom. The opposite of having power, on the other hand, is to be powerless—to be weak, slow, feeble, without ability or influence. Except among the rich and those with political influence, old age is often characterized as a time of powerlessness, with declines in physical, economic, cognitive, and social abilities. Older adults are frequently bothered by aches, pains, and other health problems; have trouble remembering things; struggle with finances; repeatedly experience the grief of losing loved ones through death or relocation; and are often displaced in work, social, and family roles. Later life is a time of increasing powerlessness and growing dependency. But is it inevitably so?

Purpose is the first word that stands prominently in the title of this book. What is it and why is it important, especially in later life? Purpose is having specific goals that we have decided are important and that we want to achieve. Our goals determine how we spend our time and resources. Not only does purpose give life direction and meaning, it is the driving force that propels us toward our goals. Purpose energizes. Purpose motivates. Purpose focuses. Purpose structures and fills a person's day.

Purpose is about having a *vision* in life. This vision is a picture of something important and significant that we see in our mind's eye, a picture of something we have not yet achieved but have decided is worth the effort to obtain.

Purpose is important because it is key to a vibrant, fulfilling, and empowering last one-third of life. Harvard psychologist William H. Sheldon said, "Happiness is essentially a state of going somewhere, wholeheartedly, one-directionally, without regret or reservation." Having purpose and vision during retirement is one of the most important determinants of mental, social, spiritual, and physical well-being in later life. Purpose is special because you can have it no matter how old you are, no matter how sick you are, no matter what your economic or social situation may be. As Benjamin Mays once said, "The tragedy of life doesn't lie in not reaching your goal. The tragedy lies in having no goal to reach." As long as you're conscious, you can have a goal.

Another reason why having purpose in retirement is so important has to do with *time*. Around the turn of the 1900s, when life expectancy was around forty-five years, people didn't spend much time in retirement. They worked until they were physically unable, experienced a short period of dependency, and then died. There was little reason to worry about how to spend time after leaving the workforce. Today, however, things have changed. If you make it to age fifty in reasonable shape, you can now expect to live to age eighty or beyond. There is a reason for this. About half the increases in life expectancy since 1970 have been due to improvements in survival after age sixty-five.[2] Because the vast majority of us today are likely to reach age sixty-five (over 80 percent), any substantial future improvements in life expectancy are likely to result from declining mortality after that age. With medical advances over the next twenty years, especially in the area of stem cell research, the average life span is likely to be extended even further—perhaps to ninety or one hundred years on average. Kenneth Manton and James Vaupel have found that while genetics have an enormous effect on susceptibility to disease due to environmental factors, the genes may be less influential than previously thought in determining human life span.[3] Quality of diet and exposure to infectious diseases and other illnesses in the first fifteen years of life may be much more important in predicting mortality later in life. If so, given the improvement in early life conditions between 1920 and 1950, life expectancies could increase over the next twenty years in the United States even more rapidly than they have in the past twenty years.[4]

The bottom line is that Americans may spend anywhere from twenty-five to forty years in retirement—almost another lifetime. Baby boomers (born between 1945 and 1967) will be the healthiest, most physically active, best-educated group of retirees in history. They will also be this country's politically most powerful group. Consider the following: by the year 2030, 47 percent of the voting population will be over age fifty and 40 percent will be over age fifty-five. These figures are based on conservative, middle series population estimates; if "high series" estimates are considered, those percentages could rise even higher.[5] Therefore, many of us will have health, knowledge, political clout, and time—plenty of time. The question is, what will we do with that time?

Existentialist philosopher and physician Karl Jaspers said, "Those who fail to realize the intrinsic meaning of their old age will only feel the sufferings of age. There is a world of difference between a man who endures, wishes, experiences, and a man who takes what is given to him, realizes it, shapes it."

Join me now on a journey to discover how to realize and shape your destiny by finding purpose in retirement. That purpose will empower and crown these years with success, significance, and meaning.

CHAPTER I

The History of Retirement

"No wise man ever wished to be younger."
—Jonathan Swift

L ET'S TAKE A CLOSER LOOK at the concept of leaving the workplace to spend life in leisure and comfort—fun in the sun, golf, and wine—the American dream for retirees. You may be surprised to learn, as I was, that the notion of spending retirement with a focus on leisure is largely a result of the marketing efforts of private entrepreneurs during the post-World War II period. In this chapter, I draw heavily on the work of Marc Freedman, president of Civic Ventures and author of *Prime Time: How Baby Boomers Will Revolutionize Retirement and Transform America.*[1] Freedman recently discovered that our society's image of "the golden years" was actually conjured up by a group of opportunistic development corporations and insurance companies only about forty to fifty years ago. These companies aggressively marketed leisure, disengagement from society, and age segregation to the American public. Their goal was clear and simple: making a profit. The view that most of us have of retirement today, therefore, is a very recent one.

Throughout most of our country's history, it was common for older adults to work productively or otherwise serve their families and communities until their health made it physically impossible to do so. In 1860, state judges were the only persons forced to retire because of age alone, and this was not true for all

states.[2] In the first edition of Webster's dictionary, published in
1928, the word "retirement" was not even associated with
advancing age. The reason? Until the latter half of the twentieth century, medicine and health care were relatively primitive
and the time after retiring from work was short and often characterized by sickness and disability, soon followed by death.
After World War II, however, things changed. Advances in
medicine and health care led both to improved health later in
life and to greater longevity. Along with better health and more
time came increased income from pensions and from new government entitlement programs such as Social Security. Indeed,
the environment was ripe for entrepreneurs to take advantage of
this new generation of increasingly mobile, financially stable
older adults with time on their hands. And take advantage of
them, they did.

❧ LEISURE ENTREPRENEURS

In his book *Prime Time*, Marc Freedman discusses the stories of
Del Webb and others whom he calls "leisure entrepreneurs."
During the past four decades, these businessmen and marketers
provided us with the popular and almost unchallenged notion of
retirement as a time for disengagement from society and as a
time for leisure. While similar smaller ventures had been taking
place in Florida and California since 1910,[3] it was the 1960
startup and subsequent growth of the Sun City retirement community in Arizona that marked the beginning of a new epic in
American history.

The opening of Sun City by the Del Webb development corporation on January 1, 1960, was a spectacular success—growing within one year to a community of 2,500 inhabitants. By
1970, it had reached 15,000; and by 1980, nearly 50,000—
becoming the seventh largest city in Arizona. Webb's organization presented a deal that few could turn down. An older person

or couple could move to Sun City and buy a three-bedroom, two-bath home for about $10,000 (in 1960 dollars). They would join a community whose values centered on activity and individuality. Even a home on the golf course (around which life revolved) only cost an additional $1,500. Of course, the community was completely age-segregated, meaning that only persons aged fifty-five or older could live there. In fact, people could be fined as much as $100 a day for illegally housing grandchildren!

Webb's $2 million investment in 1960 paid off better than he could have imagined. Over the next several decades, his development corporation would sell over 25,000 homes in Sun City and Sun City West. Sun City and the hundreds of similar age-segregated communities to follow in Arizona and Florida would transform retirement in America, making a leisured life spent in one of these communities the *symbol* of successful aging. All of this occurred within a historical context described in detail by Freedman that I will summarize here. This helps to explain why Webb's notion of retirement caught on so quickly.

❧ OLDER ADULTS IN EARLY AMERICA

In the early days of our young republic, older adults were valued by society for insight into the causes of their longevity, for moral guidance, for their knowledge about farming, and for their ability to perform domestic chores.[4] Based upon a Puritan ethic rooted in the Bible, the aged were highly respected. Long life was seen as the result of divine providence—a special blessing only given to those most worthy:

> "Rise in the presence of the aged, show respect for the elderly and revere your God. I am the LORD." —Leviticus 19:32

> "Is not wisdom found among the aged? Does not long life bring understanding?" —Job 12:12

"Gray hair is a crown of splendor; it is attained by a righteous life." —Proverbs 16:31

"[The righteous] ... will still bear fruit in old age.... "
—Psalm 92:14

This view of aging persisted for nearly two hundred years in pre-industrial America, and was responsible for the aged being highly respected and integrated into the community. Elders were seen as a resource for wisdom and, in particular, as examples for younger people.

In fact, the young even tried to look old.[5] Judges and community leaders powdered their wigs to make them silvery gray and even cut their clothes to imitate the sloping shoulders of the elderly. Paintings and sketches of the day portrayed Jesus and the angels as older, with white hair. Persons over age sixty-five, only about 2 percent of the population, were looked upon as the preservers of culture, tradition, and history. This was especially true since they often possessed the knowledge and skills needed by younger persons to succeed in a day when few people could read or write and most learning took place by apprenticeship. Early American society was guided by traditional Puritan religious values, values that were modeled and passed down by the old to the young.

Older adults were also usually in control of the finances. In an era when agriculture was the predominant source of livelihood, persons of advanced age often owned the farms that had been passed down to them through their families. Consequently, the elderly directed and supervised the work of others and could decide for themselves what kind of work they wanted to do and how long they wanted to do it.[6] The expectation of older adults was that they were to play an important role in society for as long as they were physically able, caring for small children, teaching the older children, and performing other less strenuous farm work and household chores. This positive attitude toward older adults and advancing age, however, was to radically change.

Freedman notes that the transition started in the early 1800s. This time, religious influences on society's view of older adults were not all positive. Religious groups in America at the time consisted of a wide array of predominantly Protestant sects and denominations. Each had doctrines, practices, and organizational structures that distinguished one from another. In the 1830s, however, the Second Great Awakening burst upon the scene, resulting in almost all Protestant groups taking on a deeply evangelical focus. While evangelism had always been important in Protestantism, a style led by the infamous Charles G. Finney became dominant at that time. Finney was a preacher whose fiery sermons focused on salvation and the duty of sinners to repent. Finney and his followers stressed youth, self-improvement, and progress. While adolescents had limitless possibilities in terms of salvation, the old were portrayed as long past the time of redemption. They symbolized dependency, disease, and failure, and had little future in this new culture that glorified youth. In contrast to the Puritan values that had brought honor and respect for older adults, Finney spoke against tradition and emphasized that the old had lost their chance.[7] This negative view of aging was further reinforced by changes in the workplace. As new industries and factory work began to replace agriculture, older adults became less useful because they couldn't keep up with the pace of younger workers.

By the late 1800s, instead of being viewed with reverence and honor, the elderly were seen as useless and dependent, and came to be pejoratively called "old fogeys" (a term that persists to this day). In addition to the influences of popular religious movements and economic changes, the academic professions further drove home these negative views. The professions of social work, sociology, and medicine each in their own way contributed to the new concept of old age. Value and worth were equated with productivity, which decreases with age—a fact that no one could deny. In his book *Without Consent or Contract: The Rise and Fall of American Slavery*,[8] Robert Fogel notes that the average price of male slaves in the American south peaked at age thirty-five.

Others point out, however, that while productivity decreases with age, there is no particular age at which it declines sharply.[9] Even the earnings of slaves remained positive until they reached their late seventies, suggesting that older adults could continue to work productively until advanced ages. Also, consider that almost 80 percent of all seventy-year-olds were still in the labor force in 1880. Later research in the early 1900s among factory workers would show that workers aged fifty-five to sixty-four were generally in good health and tended to spend fewer days out of work because of illness than did workers aged twenty-five to forty years.[10]

Nevertheless, the medical profession portrayed aging as an "incurable disease." Consider what Sir William Osler, a professor at Johns Hopkins and one of the founders of American medicine, had to say to his colleagues in a 1905 speech entitled "The Fixed Period." According to Osler, persons over the age of forty had little to contribute to society and stood in the way of progress:

> I have two fixed ideas well-known to my friends, harmless obsessions with which I sometimes bore them, but which have a direct bearing on this important problem. The first is the comparative uselessness of men above forty years of age. This may seem shocking, and yet read aright the world's history bears out this statement. Take the sum of human achievement in action, in science, in art, in literature—subtract the work of the men above forty, and while we should miss great treasures, even priceless treasures, we would practically be where we are today. It is difficult to

name a great and far-reaching conquest of the mind which has not been given to the world by a man on whose back the sun was still shining. The effective, moving, vitalizing work of the world is done between the ages of twenty-five and forty—these fifteen golden years of plenty, the anabolic or constructive period, in which there is always a balance in the mental bank and the credit is still good.... My second fixed idea is the uselessness of men above age sixty years of age, and the incalculable benefit it would be in commercial, political and in professional life if, as a matter of course, men stopped work at this age.... In that charming novel, *The Fixed Period*, Anthony Trollope discusses the practical advantages in modern life of a return to this ancient usage, and the plot hinges upon the admirable scene of a college into which at sixty men retired for a year of contemplation before a peaceful departure by chloroform.[11]

Apparently, Osler had forgotten the many accomplishments of Benjamin Franklin, Nathaniel Hawthorne, Daniel Webster, Abraham Lincoln, and Benjamin Disraeli after the age of sixty, or the accomplishments of Albert Einstein between age forty and his death at age seventy-six. At fifty-six years of age, when he gave this speech, Osler was not far from age sixty himself. When it came right down to it, however, he chose not to peacefully depart until the ripe old age of seventy, when he exited not from chloroform but against his will from pneumonia.

In any event, statements like this by Osler and by other respected professionals were given plenty of attention in the popular press. The impact was that by the early 1900s, older adults were being encouraged to avoid all appearance of aging by dyeing their hair, getting false teeth, and obtaining face lifts to remove wrinkles or sagging skin. The gray head, viewed as a "crown of glory" by the early Puritans, became evidence of decay, weakness, and decline. Many people who had worked hard throughout their lifetimes found themselves in "poor houses" when they became unable to work in the factories. Poor houses became the old age homes of the era. Although not meaning to, even reformers and labor leaders who were sympathetic to the plight of the elderly contributed to the growing negative view of aging by focusing the public's attention on the struggles that older adults faced.

❧ INCREASING ECONOMIC INDEPENDENCE

Gradually with the passage of time, however, older Americans began to acquire more and more economic independence. In the 1800s, the old who could no longer work became dependent on their children. With dependency came an immediate shift in status and power within the family, as the elder was replaced as head of the household. In 1880, approximately half of retired men were living with children or other relatives (compared to 5 percent today).[12] While industrialization in the late nineteenth century had its negative effects on older adults who could not work as quickly or keep up the pace of younger persons, it also had benefits.[13] For many of those who were unskilled and did not have land of their own to farm, industrialization brought real economic gains and higher salaries. Before that, wealth was possible only for a relatively small number of people who owned farms. With industrialization also came private pension plans.

In 1875, American Express began the first private pension plan; by 1900, twelve companies provided private pensions for their workers. In 1890, the pension bureau began to give out pensions to Union Army veterans who were sixty-five years or older. By the early 1900s, about one-third of men over age sixty-five were able to retire on these Civil War pensions. Like American Express, a number of large companies also began to put retirement plans in place for their workers. Offering pensions made sense. First, pensions helped companies keep high quality, experienced workers in whom they had invested considerable training. Second, offering pensions after mandatory retirement helped to minimize the costs of keeping older workers on the job. By 1930, 10 percent of all workers who received a salary were covered by pension plans.[14] In those days, however, only the wealthy, the disabled, or the few with pensions were able to retire. The median wealth of an elderly couple in 1917 ($3,000) was only about one-sixth of what it is today (corrected for inflation).[15] Consequently, the vast majority of older adults continued to work until they were physically unable to do so.

State and federal pension plans soon began to contribute to the income of older adults. In 1915, the first state-sponsored old age pensions were started in Arizona and Alaska.[16] To be eligible for these state pensions, persons had to be at least seventy, very poor, and have no financially responsible relatives. In 1935, the Social Security Act established the first national entitlement program, a federal old age pension program for persons aged sixty-five or older. The choice of age sixty-five was based on Otto von Bismarck's age of pension eligibility for members of the 1875 Prussian army (at that time in Germany the median age of death was the mid-thirties, ensuring that Bismarck would not have to offer many pensions).

Social Security was the U.S. government's response to the Great Depression, with its high youth unemployment and scarcity of jobs. The idea was that getting older adults out of the workforce would help free up jobs for young people and boost the economy. Social Security was conceived of and driven through the legislature with retirement in mind. Built into the act was that anyone who earned more than $15 a month would lose eligibility to receive benefits (a powerful motivation for those over sixty-five to stop working).[17] Furthermore, after the depression, consumption became the major solution to the country's economic problems, since by this time the productive capacities

of many American businesses had exceeded their existing mar-
kets.[18] Older adults were expected to stop producing and start
consuming during retirement in order to boost the nation's cap-
italistic economy. Since the act passed, the percentage of men
over sixty-five who continue to work has dropped precipitously.

Table 1.1. Percentage of Men Over Age 65 Still Working

Year	% working
1880	78%
1900	65%
1920	60%
1930	58%
1940	42%
1960	31%
1980	25%
2000	16%

(Source: *The Evolution of Retirement* and *Prime Time*)

Other factors contributed to the retirement trend as well.[19]
After World War II, an expansion of private and job-specific
pensions supplemented Social Security income. The Revenue
Act of 1942 provided tax incentives for companies to expand
their pension plans. By 1960, 41 percent of all wage and salaried
workers were covered. The 1950s also saw an expansion of
Social Security benefits to 10 million more persons and a 77
percent increase in benefits. In the 1960s, benefits were
extended to disabled persons aged fifty to sixty-four, and early
benefits were established for both men and women at age sixty-
two. In 1966, Medicare hospital insurance was initiated, and
benefits were increased every year between 1968 and 1973. The
Employment Retirement Security Act passed in 1974 provided
federal control to protect benefits in industry-provided pension
programs and to prevent age discrimination.

Social Security, however, remained the predominant source of income for older adults. By 1986, 81 percent of elderly households in America depended on Social Security for over half of their income (40 percent having no income from accumulated assets).[20] For the median elderly household today, Social Security is the major source of income.[21] Not surprisingly, the result of new federal and industry-sponsored programs for older adults was mass retirement.

At first, retirement—especially forced retirement—was viewed negatively by a significant proportion of the American population. Some studies indicated that 50–60 percent of those over age sixty-five would continue working if retirement could be deferred. There was even evidence in the early 1950s that many older workers were not applying for Social Security or even for benefits they might be eligible for from private pensions.[22] "Activity theory" argued that retirement was a violation of older persons' need for social and occupational integration. Soon, however, this would be replaced by "disengagement theory," which gave permission to those considering retirement to disengage and withdraw from the workplace, even arguing that retirement prevented embarrassment from "recognition of decreased abilities by others in the workgroup."[23]

After World War II, older persons in America became more and more a generation separate from the rest of a society that did not value them or their contributions. Young adults, who in the past often lived, raised their families, and worked near their parents' homes, were becoming increasingly mobile because of jobs that frequently took them to a different state or across the country. At the same time, older adults were becoming more financially secure because of pensions and entitlement programs. They were also living longer and having better health because of advances in medicine and healthier lifestyles. Because of increased finances and improved health, older adults began to rely less and less on children and other family members. It was into this "cultural vacuum," says Freedman, that the leisure entrepreneurs stepped in to offer older adults their vision of the "golden years."[24]

The first inklings of such efforts were seen in 1951 when the Corning Corporation had a roundtable discussion in which a national marketing campaign was proposed to educate people over fifty about how to enjoy leisure. The strategy was to glamorize leisure and to make every older adult feel like he or she had a right to it.[25] Insurance companies, deeply involved in the pension business, got into the act by mass advertisement of retirement preparation classes that encouraged separation from society and focused on consumption and self-preoccupation. This began the transformation of retirement into a time of rest, relaxation, and fun that every American would look forward to as the reward for a lifetime of hard labor ("the joy of being at the ballpark on a weekday afternoon").[26] Efforts were made to counteract the principle that work had value in itself, arguing that the psychological and social needs met in the workplace could be fulfilled just as well outside of it.

Ethel Percy Andrus, who founded the American Association of Retired Persons (AARP) in 1955, led an attempt to redefine the place and function of retired older adults. In order to combat the notion that mass retirement of leisure-seeking older adults would result in their becoming a burden on their children, society, and the economy, she emphasized the need for personal responsibility—for retired persons to earn this privilege by becoming productive and useful. She accepted the premise, however, that a work-centered society would have to be replaced by a leisure-centered one, and the idea of personal responsibility was more symbolic than real (called a "myth" by historian/ sociologist William Graebner)[27]. The notion of enjoyment of leisure and relinquishment of responsibility caught on much more quickly.

On August 3, 1962, the cover story of *Time* magazine featured the rapid aging of Americans who had lots of time and money but no place in society.[28] There was no mention of the value or usefulness of older Americans' skills or of the important things that they could do with their time and finances to improve the world around them and to give their lives true meaning and significance. The article talked about how Del Webb's Sun City and similar age-segregated housing developments that focused on leisure in Arizona and elsewhere were transforming America's image of retirement into a time of self-absorption and fun. This—together with the appearance of government entitlement programs and over a century of the elderly being devalued by the rest of society—was sufficient to shape America's new image of retirement. Yes, retirement in Sun City represented what older Americans were now being convinced later life ought to be like. The media, too, did their share of promoting that vision, with cover stories not only in *Time* magazine, but in multiple issues of *Newsweek, Life,* and *Reader's Digest* as well. The results were stunning. In 1951, among men receiving Social Security benefits, 3 percent retired from work to pursue leisure; in 1963, 17 percent indicated that leisure was the primary reason for retiring from work; and by 1982, nearly 50 percent of men said that they were retiring to pursue leisure.[29]

While there were positive results for some older adults who took this path, it also led many into self-absorption and prejudice, tensions with younger people, boredom, and lack of a sense that they were contributing to society and to others' lives. Today, as baby boomers look towards retirement, many want more than this—rather than allowing their talents to atrophy and their time to waste away, there is a desire to continue to contribute meaningfully to society and to invest in the next generation.

Even more important, the United States will soon not be able to afford a leisured class supported by government programs. In 1940, when Social Security benefits were first paid out, only about 43 percent of workers were covered.[30] In 1938, President

Roosevelt gave a speech to the nation in which he stated: "[T]he [Social Security] act does not offer anyone, either individually or collectively, an easy life—nor was it ever intended so to do." Social Security was never intended to provide elders with an abundant retirement, but rather to provide income sufficient to meet minimal needs. With 80 million baby boomers at the peak of their productive years, the Social Security trust fund will be generating large, temporary surpluses of over $1 trillion between 2001 and 2016.[31] This has given a sense of false security for the future. Already, there have been plans to finance the soon-to-be-depleted Medicare trust fund from these surpluses, along with funding other needs (boosting an ailing economy, bailing out states experiencing budget crises, fighting terrorism at home and abroad, helping out countries in key areas of the world, etc.).

Who will provide the funds needed by baby boomers going into retirement between 2011 and 2040, as the support ratio (number of persons aged fifteen to sixty-four divided by number of persons over age sixty-five) in the United States dwindles from five to one down to three to one?[32] The current Social Security retirement and disability program will be depleted somewhere between 2015 and 2030, and then will be supported by incoming tax revenues alone. Experts estimate that the employer-employee tax rate (plus income taxes on benefits) will slowly rise from 13 percent in 2001 to 17 percent in 2029 and higher after that.[33] Since it is likely that life expectancies over the next thirty years will increase even more than they have in the past thirty because of medical advances, this projected strain on the Social Security retirement system may be greatly underestimated. In *The Evolution of Retirement*, Dora Costa, winner of the 1998 TIAA-CREF Paul A. Samuelson Award for Outstanding Scholarly Writing on Lifelong Financial Security, notes that while recent polls indicate Americans would be willing to increase taxes to maintain Social Security and Medicare benefits, as the number of older adults needing support increases, younger taxpayers may become less and less willing to finance a system that provides a retirement characterized by recreation and leisure.[34]

❧ CONCLUSION

Older adults in early America were highly respected, a tradition based upon Puritan religious values. They served useful roles within the family, community, and society, who depended on them for those services. About 150 years ago, the view of older adults began to change—partly a result of zealous religious leaders that focused on youth, physicians that devalued aging, and well-intended political reformers trying to improve the plight of older Americans—adversely affecting how older adults were looked on by society. After private industry-sponsored pension plans and government-supported entitlement programs like Social Security and Medicare started up, the financial security of older adults began to improve. With increases in life span and improvements in health, older adults began to experience more free time after retirement. These trends created an environment that insurance companies and housing development corporations took advantage of, convincing older Americas that retirement should focus on leisure, recreation, and separation from society in age-segregated communities like Sun City. This new image of retirement came as a direct result of marketing efforts by leisure entrepreneurs focused on a new source of easy capital. The media aided these efforts by glamorizing retirement in age-segregated communities like Sun City, transforming them into the new symbol of successful aging. The upcoming generation of baby boom retirees may not be so easily convinced, nor may the younger taxpayers who will have to support their retirement.

❧ CHAPTER 2

Myths of Retirement

"Experience is a hard teacher —
she gives the test first, and the lesson afterwards."
—*Vernon Sanders*

I N THE LAST CHAPTER I examined the history of retirement as it evolved in America since colonial days. It appears that the image of retirement viewed by many today is at least partly based on myth. Other myths about old age and retirement also abound in society. Myths are popular beliefs that many of us accept as facts, yet their truth remains elusive due to a lack of solid evidence to substantiate them. While some might acknowledge that a particular belief is untrue, their lives suggest otherwise—they live as if the myth were fact. This chapter reviews twenty common myths about retirement and discusses whether they are based on fact or fiction.

Myth 1.

Once people retire from work, they will be able to relax and enjoy the fruits of their lifelong labor without concern or worry.
Fact: Results of a recent study found that compared to older adults working full time, retirees' daily activities had more variety and autonomy and were more manageable. However, the study also revealed that lives of retirees were less fulfilling.[1] In another study, retirement was associated with a diminished sense of control, less well-being, and greater depression—except for a

short period immediately following retirement, which appeared to represent a "honeymoon" phase of being out of the labor force.[2] Investigators concluded that work was empowering and that retirement led to lower levels of well-being.

Explanation: When challenges and people-problems at work are no longer a worry, other problems of a different nature soon begin to surface—problems with spouse, family, and friends, problems with health and physical functioning, and sometimes problems with not having enough to do. At no other time does questioning the meaning of life become more intense. While it is certainly not always so, retirement can be a time of identity crisis.

Myth 2.

Things will get better after retiring to a relaxing life of entertainment, watching TV, eating and drinking, going to bed early, and getting up late—everything that work prevented.

Fact: Lack of attention to health and lifestyle in later life can lead to worse mental and physical health and ultimately to a shortened retirement.[3]

Explanation: Retirement to an inactive lifestyle of self-indulgence often results in weight gain, excessive alcohol use, chronic fatigue, and physical deconditioning. This almost always leads to dissatisfaction with life, depression, and loss of meaning and sense of usefulness. A disciplined lifestyle is more important in retirement than at any other time, since body metabolism slows, making weight gain easier, reducing energy, and requiring careful attention to health habits to maintain pre-retirement health.

Myth 3.

After retirement, husband and wife will finally be happy and enjoy life together.

Fact: In a study of couples' adaptation to the husband's retirement, investigators found that over half the women reported problems of "impingement" because husbands were spending more time at home.[4] In a national sample of 1,183 married persons, it was found that leaving a high-stress job improves marital quality, whereas retirement caused by poor health (resulting in role reversals) or that reduces social interactions tends to worsen marital quality.[5] A more indepth study by researchers of ten couples in which both partners had been retired for six to eighteen months found that changes in roles and identity with retirement were significant stressors.[6] After retiring, these couples tended to communicate their thoughts rather than their feelings to one another. Thoughts tended to center around the children. With more contact, spouses became increasingly aware of their partners' faults. Compared to wives, husbands tended to be more satisfied in retirement. Interestingly, hobbies and time spent together did not change significantly following retirement, suggesting that most couples attempted to maintain continuity between retirement and previous lifestyles. In one of the largest studies to date, 2,076 married adults aged fifty-five or over were surveyed on how retirement affected their marital satisfaction. Negative effects were observed when husbands retired if their wives continued working (especially conflicts over household division of labor). Investigators concluded that "there was no indication of any beneficial impact of retirement on the marital satisfaction of either husbands or wives."[7]

Explanation: Retirement often has a powerful and pervasive influence on marital quality—those influences can be good or bad depending on the circumstances of retirement and the relationship of the couple. In circumstances where husband and wife lived independent lives prior to retirement (particularly if both were employed) and did not have a close marital relationship, then retirement will result in more time spent in close contact. This can require a major adjustment for both spouses.

Husband and wife may have different interests and different dreams about what they imagined retirement would be like.

Myth 4.
Circumstances in retirement will determine happiness.
Fact: While good health, sufficient income, and the ability to control life are important predictors of well-being during retirement, there is not a one-to-one correlation.[8]
Explanation: Many people with health problems, low income, and less than ideal living circumstances experience well-being and happiness in retirement. These people tend to be those with positive attitudes,[9] strong religious faith,[10] and active social relationships,[11] especially if they are involved in volunteer work.[12]

Myth 5.
Having plenty of money is necessary to a happy retirement.
Fact: Income is a weak predictor of happiness.[13]
Explanation: Although wealthier people tend to be happier than those who are poor, influences of income on happiness occur primarily at low incomes; once basic needs are met, there is no proportional increase in happiness with further increases in income. It is one of those eternal, nonnegotiable laws that wealth does not produce happiness—happiness comes as a natural consequence of worthy actions.

Jesus said: "It is easier for a camel to go through the eye of a needle than for a rich man to enter the kingdom of God" (Mark 10:25).

Muhammad said: "Wealth and sons are allurements of the life of this world: But the things that endure, good deeds, are best in the sight of thy Lord, as rewards, and best as [the foundation for] hopes" (Sura 18:46).

Buddha said: "Riches make most people greedy, and so are like caravans lurching down the road to perdition. Any possession that increases the sin of selfishness or does nothing to confirm one's wish to renounce what one has is nothing but a drawback in disguise" (Jatakamala 5.5, 15).

They can't all be wrong.

Myth 6.

Planning for retirement is not necessary. The retired can live on Social Security.

Fact: Someone once said, "He who trusts all things to chance makes a lottery of his life." Social Security will provide about a third of what an older person will need in retirement. Consider that the median yearly household income for persons in the United States in 1999 was $40,816 (most recent data available).[14] In 2001, the average Social Security check for retired workers in the United States was $845 per month ($10,140 a year) or $1,410 per month ($16,920 a year) for a married couple.[15] This means that the average married couple who retires and relies entirely on Social Security will experience a drop in income of nearly 60 percent (from $41,000 to $17,000 a year). While this is still six times more income than World War I-era older adults had during their retirement years, it can create a major adjustment problem if not anticipated.

And it doesn't appear that Americans today are planning much for retirement. According to a December 26, 2001, business report on CNN, "U.S. consumers have outspent their incomes and acquired record debt since the late 1990s.... Another factor has been Americans' savings rate—the net of what we earn versus what we spend. It has sunk to historical lows in the past two years, averaging about 1 percent in 2000 and most recently 0.9 percent in November 2001, according to David Wyss (Standard & Poor's chief economist). The savings rate in 1994 was 9 percent."[16]

Explanation: As noted in the last chapter, Social Security surpluses are expected to be large for a while due to the large population of contributing workers and, up until 2001, a booming economy. The government is now tapping that surplus to bolster national security, defense, and other domestic programs. Will it be able to continue to dole out checks each month to maintain a comfortable standard of living for retired persons during the next few decades? Better start saving now, and remember the old saying, "Love of money is the root of half the evil in the world; and the lack of money is the root of the other half."

Myth 7.

Don't worry about physical health, since there's not much that can be done about it anyway.

Fact: Older adults who exercise, pay attention to diet and weight, keep their stress levels down, and see physicians for regular medical checkups are healthier and happier than those who do not.[17]

Explanation: Aging is associated with normal declines in physiological reserves, so that disease or illness has more potential to overcome the body's defenses. Attention to activities that maintain physical health helps to preserve those reserves in body systems like the heart, lungs, muscles, bones, and internal organs. With good physical health often comes good mental health and satisfaction with life; among those in poor health, depression and anxiety are common and widespread. When physical activity is combined with stimulating social interactions, overall greater well-being is the likely result.[18]

Myth 8.

Retirement always leads to worse health, mental decline, and unhappiness.

Fact: Retirement does not always lead to worse health or loss of well-being.[19] People who stay physically fit, socially involved, and engaged in meaningful activities often experience improvements in well-being and health following retirement.

Explanation: Those who retire to an inactive lifestyle of self-indulgence and consumption experience declines in health and well-being after retirement, particularly over the long term. While the short-term experience of not having to work anymore may be very enjoyable, as noted before, this honeymoon period doesn't last long for many retired people. That loss of enjoyment, however, is not inevitable.

Myth 9.

It is natural to disengage from society and withdraw from community involvement as one grows older.

Fact: Older people who disengage from society or withdraw from social interactions often do so because they are depressed, angry, or otherwise emotionally distressed and disappointed, having lost vision and purpose for their lives. Disengagement is not part of normal aging.

Explanation: As noted in Chapter 1, there was a popular concept of normal aging in the 1950s and 1960s called "disengagement theory." This replaced, and then was later replaced by, a theory arguing that staying active and involved was a better indicator of normal aging than was disengagement (known as "activity theory"). Activity theory emphasizes the need to find substitutes for activities no longer possible because of health, financial, or social losses. This theory, however, has been criticized, because well-being in later life is not so much determined by the number of activities or number of social contacts, but rather by the level of social integration and perceived quality of relationships.[20] As Henry David Thoreau said, "It is not enough to be industrious; so are the ants. The question is: What are you industrious about?"

Myth 10.

People don't need others to be happy. The most fulfilling life is one of independence and self-sufficiency.

Fact: People do need other people to maintain their happiness and well-being, especially when sickness or other kinds of losses occur.[21] One of the strongest predictors of well-being at this time is how much social support a person receives from family and friends. Studies have shown that social participation is particularly important for predicting life satisfaction after retirement, even more so than for persons still able to derive enjoyment from work activity.[22] Being a friend to others is also a strong predictor of happiness in later life.[23] Level of social support and social activity is not only associated with better mental health, but is also a strong predictor of physical health and survival.[24]

Explanation: Humans are social animals with a deep need for companionship, interaction, and intimacy. Lack of adequate socialization evokes a feeling called loneliness. Loneliness and social isolation have been repeatedly associated with worse mental and physical health.[25] Walt Disney once said, "You can dream, create, design, and build the most wonderful place in the world, but it requires people to make the dream a reality." People need people to be happy—even introverts.

Myth 11.

Retirement that focuses only on leisure and pleasure (receiving, consuming, being entertained) is satisfying and produces happiness.

Fact: Recall from the last chapter that among men receiving Social Security benefits, nearly 50 percent indicated in 1982 that they retired in order to pursue leisure (a seventeen-fold increase from 3 percent in 1951). After sleep, the most common activity that persons over age sixty-five spend their time on is recreation (35 percent of their time—a figure that is 50 percent greater than for persons under age sixty-five).[26] Nearly one-half of elders' free time is spent watching television. This prompted one group of leisure time experts to comment, "The lives of most seniors who fill out our time diaries seem to revolve around the television set."[27] A life of self-absorption is never a happy life.

Explanation: People tend to accommodate emotionally to whatever situation they find themselves in—whether it be the experience of pleasure or pain. It's like going to sleep on the beach. At first one hears the waves crashing against the sand. But pretty soon, the waves aren't heard consciously anymore because the mind has grown accustomed to them. Similarly, give anyone a steady diet of pleasure—and only pleasure—and it will quickly lose its delight and become boring, even irritating. Humans are made that way—they crave diversity and change (and yet at the same time resist it). Variety is truly the spice of life. The most common responses to incessant routine or absence of change are: 1) alcohol, 2) over-activity, and 3) possessive relationships. Alcohol drowns out the disappointment and disillusionment that boredom causes. Activity distracts the person from a life that lacks meaning. Relationships become exclusive and clinging when used to dispel the loneliness and sense of isolation resulting from a life of self-centeredness.

Myth 12.

It is more blessed to receive (be a consumer of leisure) than to give.
Fact: As the data accumulate, it is becoming more and more evident that people who reach out to others during retirement experience greater well-being than those who do not. In a nationwide study of older adults, investigators at the Institute of Social Research at the University of Michigan found that those who gave assistance to others experienced significantly greater feelings of personal control and well-being than older adults who did not provide support to others.[28] In another study, 158 retired persons were categorized into four groups: givers, receivers, givers and receivers, and neither givers nor receivers.[29] The groups were followed and their health outcomes assessed. At the end of six months, givers had significantly better physical health. Those who both gave and received had greater self-esteem and well-being. Persons in the group that neither gave

nor received help from others experienced the worst physical and mental health over time.

Explanation: Health and well-being are associated with giving to others and also, to some extent, with a willingness to receive from others. In the end, those who neither give to nor receive from others often end up neither healthy nor happy. Social science research[30] demonstrates this principle, which is rooted in all major religious traditions around the world. Especially in later life, it is better to give than to receive—and it may often be necessary to do both.

Myth 13.

Older workers are not as useful and cannot work as effectively as younger workers.

Fact: Although productivity levels and speed decline with age, older workers can work as effectively as younger workers. In addition, they have lower absenteeism rates, less job turnover, and lower rates of accidents than do younger workers.[31]

Explanation: Compared to younger workers, older workers tend to have slower reaction times, take longer to learn new tasks, and have reduced physical speed.[32] Many jobs, however, do not depend on reaction time or speed of learning, but rather on experience and judgment—which older adults have plenty of.

Myth 14.

More people are volunteering today in the United States than in the past.

Fact: Both the percentage of adults who volunteer and the average time spent volunteering has declined in the United States (see chapter 5).[33]

Explanation: Americans are spending less and less time volunteering to help others. The reason for this decline is unknown but is interesting, given the increased attention paid to spirituality in this country. The form of spirituality that is growing, however, tends to be self-centered, not other-focused. The spirituality of this new age stresses personal empowerment and de-emphasizes institutional religion or attention to social needs.[34] Other societal trends further reinforce such changes. The American lifestyle often requires that both spouses work in order to maintain an adequate household income. Any time that's left over tends to be spent resting or with family, not on volunteer work.

Myth 15.

Most older adults in the United States do volunteer work after they retire.

Fact: The majority of older adults do no volunteer work at all.[35] Even after controlling for health and socioeconomic status, increasing age is not associated with increased volunteering.[36] Nor do those who are not volunteering want to do so. Only approximately one in ten older adults who are not employed or doing volunteer work would like to volunteer if asked.[37]

Explanation: If people do not volunteer time to help others before retirement, they are unlikely to begin doing so after retirement. Instead, they tend to seek continuity in their behaviors before and after retirement. Only a minority of retired persons who are not already volunteering says that they would consider volunteering if the opportunity arose.

Myth 16.

There are no opportunities for retired people to get involved.

Fact: Many opportunities exist for motivated retired people to contribute their time and talents to improving the world around them, including both paid and unpaid activities. The website of Civic Ventures lists eighteen volunteer opportunities for the retired along with information on how to contact the organizations. The list includes Experience Corps, Corporation for National Service, National Senior Service Corps, Volunteers in Medicine, Elderhostel, Habitat for Humanity, Environmental

Alliance for Senior Involvement, Hope for Children, Foster Grandparents Program, Peace Corps, Troops to Teachers, Service Corps of Retired Executives, National Retiree Volunteer Coalition, Points of Light Foundation, America's Promise, and American Association of Retired Persons, to name just a few.[38] Informal opportunities to volunteer are even more plentiful— consider all the people living alone in the community who need companionship or someone to do odd jobs around the house that they are unable to perform.

Explanation: There are many, many needs in this world (physical needs, emotional needs, spiritual needs, needs for wisdom, skill, and experience), and those who are retired have the ability to meet those needs. Disengaging from society is a waste of our God-given talents and resources that were divinely intended to help others.

Myth 17.

Older persons who retire are physically too disabled or ill to volunteer.
Fact: Almost 80 percent of Americans aged sixty-five or over in 1994 had no physical disability,[39] and the percentage of those with no disability is increasing every year.[40]

Explanation: Advances in medicine and increased attention to lifestyle are producing a healthier older population than ever before. This is particularly true for aging baby boomers. Thus, health problems should not prevent most retired persons from volunteering. Even those with chronic illness and physical disability can volunteer in ways that do not physically stress them—such as providing telephone support to encourage others with similar problems.

Myth 18.

Most older persons have memory problems, disorientation, or dementia that prevents them from productive activity.
Fact: Only about 10 percent of those over age sixty-five experi-

ence dementia or severe mental illness that prevents them from engaging in productive activities.[41]

Explanation: Most retired persons do not have significant disturbances of emotion, concentration, or memory that would prevent them from volunteering or providing practical types of support to others. In fact, there is evidence that volunteering may help to prevent emotional problems in later life and increase quality of life.[42] Furthermore, remaining mentally and physically active by contributing to society in meaningful ways is likely to be one of the best ways to preserve memory and cognitive function as people grow older.[43]

Myth 19.

Older adults have few economic resources.

Fact: Remember from the last chapter that the median non-housing wealth of heads of households aged sixty to sixty-five today has increased by sixfold from what it was in 1917 (controlling for the effects of inflation).[44] In 1999, after including government benefits, only 8.4 percent of persons over age sixty-five had income levels below the poverty level, compared to 9.9 percent for adults of all ages.[45] Whether baby boomers will enjoy similar economic prosperity during retirement—given their low rate of saving, increasing debt, and the predicted strains on Social Security ahead—is not known.

Explanation: Private pension plans, interest on savings, capital gains, part-time work, and government benefits (Social Security) provide most of the income for older adults today. If government benefits were not included, however, the figure of 8 percent of older adults living below the poverty level would rise to 48 percent. The median annual income in 1999 of a household headed by a person aged sixty-five or older was $22,812 (one-half that of households headed by persons aged fifty-five to sixty-four [$44,597] or aged forty-five to fifty-four [$56,917]).[46] The cost of living, however, tends to be lower for retired persons than for those who are working because they have fewer pay-ments (house and auto are usually paid off) and have fewer costs involved in raising and educating children (children have left the home). As a result, the vast majority of today's elderly in the United States have economic resources that are sufficient to meet their own needs and more.

Myth 20.

Once a person accumulates enough to retire and is economically secure, then he or she will start giving money to charitable causes.

Fact: In general, the rate and amount of giving does not increase after people retire. Among those who contributed money to charitable organizations in 1998, the average percentage of per-sonal income contributed by persons of all ages was 2.1 percent. The comparable figure for persons aged fifty-five to sixty-four was 1.9 percent; for persons aged sixty-five to seventy-four it was 2 percent.[47]

Explanation: Just as with volunteering, giving tends to remain stable with aging. People who were givers in young adulthood and middle age continue to be givers in their retirement years. The same applies to those who do not give to charitable causes; after they retire, there is no evidence that giving increases regardless of economic security. Humans are creatures of habit— the habit of giving is best developed early, since it seldom emerges for the first time in later life.

❧ CONCLUSION

Myths about aging and retirement abound. Systematic research has helped to dispel many of these myths, which are often half-truths or misperceptions of the truth. Retirement solves some problems but raises others. While aging is associated with declines in some areas, new possibilities and potentials also emerge. Those possibilities and potentials result from the wisdom and experience gained by age, by the additional time available, and because fewer responsibilities constrain that time. In the chapters to follow, I will examine in greater depth how having purpose and goals during this critical time called retirement can give meaning, significance, health, and power—and discuss further exactly *what kind of purpose* actually does this. First, however, I'd like to take a closer look at the dark side of retirement—what happens if time and talents are wasted or squandered on idleness.

CHAPTER 3

Retirement Can Be Deadly

"There is little hope for democracy if the hearts of men and women in democratic societies cannot be touched by a call to something greater than themselves." —Margaret Thatcher

ETIREMENT does not always lead to health problems and a shortened life span. But does it ever do so? Can retirement be deadly for some, leading to a rapid decline both mentally and physically? Is there a dark side to this period of life that seeks to snag unwary travelers? What is the nature of that dark side, and how can it be avoided? In this chapter, I will look at how much time Americans are likely to spend in retirement, explore the negative effects of retirement on mental health and well-being, examine how emotional experiences during retirement influence the physical body, and finally, identify characteristics of retirement that make it satisfying, fulfilling, and health-enhancing.

꙳ THE EXPANDING RETIREMENT YEARS

Each successive generation is spending more and more time in retirement. The present generation of older adults will live longer than any previous generation in recorded history, and the next generation after that will live even longer. Nearly one-half of all people who have *ever* survived to the age of sixty-five are alive today.[1] In the last hundred years, life span has increased more than in the previous five thousand years. Despite improvements in health and longevity, many workers retire young. By age sixty-two, only 44 percent of men and 24 percent of women in the United States today are still working full-time.² Eligibility for employer-provided retirement benefits can begin as young as age fifty in some corporations and is widespread by age fifty-five. Eligibility for Social Security benefits starts at age sixty-two. This means that Americans will be spending a long time in retirement—a very long time.

Living long, however, is not the same as living well. Nor is it the same as living healthy, independent, and pain free. What most people really want is not just more years to live, but years that are vigorous and healthy. The U.S. Department of Health and Human Services publication *Healthy People 2010* describes a measure called "years of healthy life," which is the difference between life expectancy and time spent with chronic or acute health limitations.³ According to government studies, in 1996 Americans lived an average 64.2 years of healthy life. Healthy life also extends beyond the physical to include the emotional, social, and spiritual. This is everyone's ultimate goal—more years of healthy life.

What is key to expanding years of healthy life? Will retirement to a life of leisure, relaxation, and self-absorption in an age-segregated community of one's peers, reflecting the vision of the "golden years" described in chapter 1, do it? Scientific research has indeed uncovered some fascinating findings in this regard. There is growing evidence that an inactive, disengaged, self-focused retirement can lead to increased health problems, and that a purpose-filled life of volunteerism, generosity, and service to others can help to prevent them.

❧ RETIREMENT AND MENTAL HEALTH

In his widely read book *Why Survive?*, renowned geriatric medicine specialist Robert Butler describes what he calls the "retirement syndrome." It is a succinct description of how retirement can affect the mind and psyche of some individuals.[4]

People who retire do not automatically develop declining mental and physical health. What social-science studies we have indicate such generalizations tend to be a fallacy. Yet there are clinical indications that some individuals are badly affected (reconciliation of clinical experience and social-science data tends to be difficult since individuals experiencing difficulty are often buried in the larger generalized social-science data). Men and women who are otherwise perfectly healthy sometimes develop headaches, gastrointestinal symptoms, oversleeping, irritability, nervousness and lethargy in connection with retirement. These conditions may manifest themselves before retirement takes place; they can heighten with the confusion of roles, activities and changes in the structure of one's life that develops at the time of retirement; they worsen if one does not find a satisfactory lifestyle and work supplements after retirement. Without the customary defensive value of work, old emotional conflict may re-emerge, especially if one has been a workaholic—addicted to work. *Without purpose* [emphasis added], a sense of inadequacy can evolve; and apathy and inertia.[5]

Writing as a social gerontologist, S. J. Miller also depicts retirement as a time of "identity crisis" for some people. He notes that retirement can be degrading because there is an unspoken implication that a retired person can no longer play the role that he or she once did on the job. The identity received from an occupation invades all other areas of a person's life, including that of father and head of household, friend, and even social status during leisure activities. Self-identity based on work is related to deeply rooted values regarding what is legitimate as a source of social worth.

Leisure roles have a difficult time replacing work as a source of self-esteem because they are typically not supported by societal norms (despite vigorous marketing efforts by leisure entrepreneurs over the past five decades). Furthermore, leisure as a legitimate source of self-esteem will likely become less and less valid in the future as our society (and the world) begins to feel the economic pinch caused by aging populations needing support and care. Consequently, the only kinds of leisure that are truly effective in providing identity are work substitutes that result in the production of something worthwhile.

If the stigma of an implied inability to perform carries over into the individual's other roles in life, identity breakdown—in which former claims to prestige and positive self-concept can no longer hold up—may occur. As self-concept plummets, the retired person begins to feel embarrassed, wishes to withdraw from others, and retreats inward. Unless pursuits can be identified to adequately replace work as a source of identity and self-esteem, a sense of despair and loss of usefulness can ensue. Again, the result is similar to that described by Butler.

Miller implies that one way to solve the problem is to create an ethic in society that would make full-time leisure an acceptable and worthwhile role. This has already happened to some extent since he articulated his position over thirty-five years ago. With more and more older persons retiring to a life of leisure, we are beginning to expect it and even feel entitled to it. That ethic, however, is about to change.

A recent book authored by Peter Peterson, secretary of commerce under President Nixon, describes the impact that global aging is likely to have soon. That impact includes the possibility of a bankrupt society due to a vast population of leisure-consuming, self-indulgent older adults with an "entitlement ethic."[6] According to Peterson, there is an expanding group of retired persons who are healthy though inactive, needing expensive social services, largely dependent on the government for their income, and who are intent on living a life of leisure and on doing so at the expense of the rest of society. He is concerned that this trend will soon erupt into social warfare between the young (who will be increasingly expected to pay the bill) and the old. All of these trends bode poorly for the self-image and sense of self-worth of older adults who wish to retire to a life of leisure and rest, particularly those who are not forced to do so because of health problems.

Research backs up the negative impact that retirement can have on mental health. No doubt, this depends on the kind of job one had during the work years. Retirement is more likely to precipitate emotional problems or identity crises in persons whose jobs were fulfilling and ego- enhancing. This is especially true for executives and high-level managers, business owners, and other professionals whose work has consumed much of their time and interests. Even low-status jobs, however, can be fulfilling in one way or another, especially from a social stand-point.

After comparing four groups of older persons including: 1) those living at home, 2) patients in a mental hospital, 3) patients in a geriatric hospital, and 4) residents of a home for the aged, British psychiatrist Maurice Silverman concluded that prolonged inactivity following retirement from work and absence of positive interests are conducive to both mental and physical health problems.[7] The effect was particularly notice-able among men. Women tended to experience mental health symptoms at a later age. This, he explained, was because women were much less likely to be compulsorily retired from their reg-ular work compared to men.

In a 1949 study of seventy-five people between the ages of fifty and eighty years, subjects were interviewed to determine their attitudes toward occupational curtailment, modification, and retirement.[8] Approximately two-thirds were engaged in reg-ular activities. A desire to continue to work arose out of a need for self-respect, to escape self-preoccupation, depression, and restlessness. This was particularly true for people who had been dismissed from their jobs without warning. Other studies have shown that women who work at low occupational status jobs are particularly vulnerable to emotional problems after they retire.[9]

There is also evidence of an increased suicide risk, especially within the first month after retirement. For that reason, health professionals have been warned to be vigilant for such a possibility among recently retired persons.[10]

❧ RETIREMENT AND SOCIAL RELATIONSHIPS

Social adjustment after retirement can also be challenging. Difficulties with adjustment may force some people back to work, and studies have shown that retirees who do return to work have higher levels of social adjustment than unemployed retirees.[11] Other studies have shown that employment in the retirement years is related to larger social networks and indirectly, through this relationship, to better physical health.[12]

No doubt, it is more difficult to maintain relationships with friends at work after retirement. A study examined differences in coworker support between retirees and those who were currently employed.[13] Fewer retirees than workers indicated that coworkers were friends, and retirees almost never discussed their personal problems with former coworkers. Other research has demonstrated that elderly men who take early retirement have particular difficulty maintaining social relationships.[14] These findings suggest a discontinuity of friendship networks from active employment to retirement.

Other research suggests friendships within age-segregated retirement communities may not be as fulfilling as friendships maintained outside of these communities.[15] Examining the extent to which social support from friends both within and outside of a retirement community was associated with depression, investigators found that social support from friends within the retirement community failed to have a significant effect on preventing the development of depression. In contrast, social support from friends living elsewhere was a consistent predictor of low levels of depression. In addition, perceived quality of relationships was higher for friends living outside of the retirement community.

Involvement in meaningful activities during retirement may help to counteract the negative mental and social consequences of leaving the workforce. In a study of retired government employees, activities connected with an occupation, hobbies, interactions with friends, and volunteer organizations were associated with greater life satisfaction.[16] As suggested by Robert Butler and S. J. Miller, retirement can also have a negative impact on a person's sense of usefulness. This fact seems borne out by the results of a national survey conducted by a Harris poll, which found that the majority of older adults in the United States experience a loss of usefulness after retirement.[17] Humans have a psychological need to be needed, and fulfilling that need may be a key to successful aging and to psychological adjustment in retirement.

❧ THE MIND AFFECTS THE BODY

Scientists are discovering that psychological factors, emotions, and the quality of social relationships can directly impact a person's physical body and health status.[18] Psychological stress, anxiety, and depression have been shown to impair immune responses, delay wound healing, increase susceptibility to infectious diseases, and increase risk for cardiovascular problems leading to heart attacks, high blood pressure, and stroke (see chapter 8). Furthermore, social support and strong friendship networks appear to counteract these negative effects on physical health, as does a sense of purpose and meaning.[19]

If retirement increases emotional stress or social isolation or results in a sense of uselessness, there are known biological pathways by which retirement could adversely affect physical health. This may be particularly true for older adults whose immune and cardiovascular systems are already compromised because of aging or disease. Furthermore, if a physical health problem was a reason for retirement, then the act of retirement itself (if stressful) could weaken the body's ability to fight off the illness and thereby lead to a downward cycle of mental and physical deterioration. In an eye-opening piece written for the *Harvard Business Review*, Leland Bradford asks, "Can you survive your retirement?"[20] He notes that unless preparations are made, feelings of emptiness and emotional strain can overwhelm the new retiree—leading to emotional, relational, and physical problems, which he then describes with graphic examples.

❦ RETIREMENT AND PHYSICAL HEALTH

Both clinical observations and scientific research show that retirement *for some people* results in a decline of physical health. Consider a 1980 report entitled "Retirement and Coronary Mortality" published in the prestigious British medical journal *The Lancet*.[21] The article discusses a study conducted at Harvard Medical School's Channing Laboratory in Boston that was also presented at the American Health Association's annual meeting. The study suggested that retirement could lead to fatal coronary heart disease. Five hundred sixty-eight men who had died of a heart attack in 1973 and 1974 were matched by age and neighborhood of residence with 568 living men (controls) identified through systematic household surveys. Information was obtained from the wives of both the dead men and from the control subjects.

Results indicated that retired men had a risk of dying from coronary artery disease that was 2.9 times higher than employed men (95 percent confidence intervals ranged from 1.9 times as high to 4.9 times as high). After adjusting further for age and history of previous myocardial infarction, this reduced the relative risk of dying to 1.8, still a significant difference. Compared to employed men, those who were retired were 80 percent more likely to have died from a heart attack—a substantial risk. The findings from this study were corroborated by preliminary reports from a study at Duke University of 1,500 patients undergoing coronary angiography, which also found that not working was a predictor of greater mortality from heart disease.[22] The authors explained the findings as being due to either an adverse effect of retirement that led to coronary artery disease or to the disabling effect of coronary artery disease that led to retirement. Because of the nature of the study, direction of causation could not be determined.

In a report from Sweden, researchers in the Department of Orthopaedics, Malmo General Hospital, found that the incidence of hip fractures in men fifty to sixty-four increased significantly between the 1950s and the 1980s.[23] Among the significant predictors of hip fracture were alcohol misuse, living alone, and early retirement. Investigators concluded that excessive alcohol use and suspected physical inactivity in this group of middle-aged men probably predisposed them to osteoporosis and increased fracture risk.

Researchers in Spain have reported similar results. As part of the TURVA retirement project, investigators followed 339 urban and rural residents over age sixty for a period of four years.[24] During the study, twenty-four subjects died. Predictors of mortality included poor mental health, financial problems, dissatisfaction with life, marital problems, and excessive leisure time. This study suggests that psychological and social problems in retirement—along with having excessive leisure time—may increase the risk of early mortality.

Jim House and colleagues reported results from a study of over

2,750 men and women living in Tecumseh, Michigan, who were followed for twelve years.[25] They examined the effects of social relationships and activity on longevity and health. While the study did not specifically focus on retirement, one of the findings was an association between mortality and the leisure activity of "watching TV." Women who spent large amounts of free time watching television experienced a significant increase in their risk of dying during the study period. Recall from chapter 2 that nearly one-half of older adults' free time is spent watching television—more than any other age group.[26]

Not all studies find worsening health problems or increased mortality following retirement. D. J. Ekerdt and colleagues studied 229 retirees and 409 workers ages fifty-five to seventy-three years who participated in the Veterans Administration normative aging project in Boston.[27] They compared pre- to post-retirement changes in physical health among male retirees with those that occurred in men of similar age who continued working. Physical health was rated on a four-point scale based on medical examinations. After controlling for age and excluding men who retired because of illness or disability, investigators found no significant difference in health change between retirees and continuing workers. They concluded that the event of retirement does not increase the risk of health deterioration.

 Timo Niemi investigated the effects of retirement on mortality among 1,176 men retired on an old-age pension.[28] The basis for retirement in all cases was age, not poor health. Retirement did not have any long-term or short-term effects on mortality in this Scandinavian study. However, among retired men whose spouse died during the follow-up (174 out of 939 men), there was a significant short-term increase in mortality.[29] Compared to retirees whose spouses were still alive, there was an increased rate of death among bereaved retirees from cardiovascular disease and cancer during the first six months after the spouse's death. More recent research from the Normative Aging Study at Arizona State University supports this finding by showing that employment appears to prevent the negative effects on health caused by bereavement.[30] For 511 older men in this study, being employed prevented physical health deterioration both at the twelve-month follow-up and at the twenty-four to thirty-six month follow-up after bereavement.

In order to disentangle the relationship between health and retirement, researchers at the Gerontology Institute at the University of Massachusetts in Boston examined the association between health status and work behavior among men aged fifty-five to sixty-nine to better understand the conditions under which health is most strongly associated with retirement.[31] In this study, poor health was a particularly strong predictor of retirement among men with working wives, men who were younger, and men with limited non-work financial resources. Certainly, a major confounder of the retirement-health relationship is the need to continue working for financial reasons.

While many studies do not find that retirement leads to worse physical health, this hypothesis has not yet been rigorously tested. Such a test would require a clinical trial. In such an experiment, a large sample of working men in their mid- to late-fifties would have to be randomly assigned to either retirement or continued employment, and then their health monitored carefully over ten to twenty years. While such a study would be expensive to carry out, it might provide vital information to help guide the decisions of millions of prospective retirees for decades to come.

One thing is more certain. If retirement leads to inactivity, then health problems and greater mortality will likely result. Physical inactivity has been shown to be a strong predictor of future mortality in numerous studies.[32] For example, researchers at the Cooper Institute in Dallas, Texas, followed nearly twenty-five thousand men over a ten-year period to examine predictors of mortality. The average age of subjects at the start of the study was forty-four years.[33] The mortality rate was much higher among men with low physical fitness due to inactivity. When older subjects have been studied, the results are the same. In an eight-year study of 1,109 persons aged sixty-five to eighty-four years who were living independently in central Finland, lack of physical activity was again a strong risk factor for further disability and death.[34]

❧ IMPLICATIONS FOR HEALTH IN RETIREMENT

Writing in the 1930s, French churchman Ernest Dimnet noted: "Very busy people always find time for everything. People with immense leisure find time for nothing." Over-involvement with self, a focus on leisure and inactivity, and reduction in social interactions after retirement may result in psychological and physical problems. In contrast, staying physically and mentally active, avoiding excessive alcohol use, smoking, and overeating, and remaining involved with others in social interactions consistently predict better health during retirement. Research also suggests that participating in altruistic activities like volunteer work may increase well-being, health, and longevity.[35] This latter point is perhaps best demonstrated in a study conducted by a life insurance company of policyholders whose average age was over one hundred years. Policyholders were asked what was the most important thing they learned during their long lives.[36] The most common response by these centenarians was "to love your neighbor as yourself."

Such an attitude may have helped to free these long-livers from guilt, anger, hatred, suspicion, anxiety, resentment, and other negative emotions that could have adversely affected their immune and cardiovascular systems. Caring concern for the needs of others may indeed impact health. A study by psychologist David McClelland found that people who simply watched a film of Mother Teresa providing care for the poor in India enjoyed significant positive changes in their immune function.[37] It makes sense, then, that ignoring the needs of others and focusing entirely on one's own pleasures and satisfactions are likely to have the opposite effect on good health.

❧ CONCLUSION

The years spent in retirement are likely to continue to increase, providing more and more free time. There is evidence that retirement for some leads to an identity crisis, to emotional problems, and sometimes to fewer social interactions of lesser quality. These effects on mental and social health can also influence physical health because there is such a close connection between the emotions and the biological processes that maintain the physical body. While studies do not show that retirement results in a significant worsening of health for all people, it is likely that retirement does adversely affect the health of some individuals. This is particularly true for those whose work has been important to their identity, use of time, and social relationships, for those who have not prepared for the event of retirement by developing activities during the work years that can be continued after retirement, and for those who have retired to an inactive lifestyle focused on leisure and self-preoccupation. Spiritual health, too, may be affected during retirement if the focus is entirely on the self. Samuel Logan Brengle, whose writings influenced the start of the Salvation Army, said it plainly: "Faith is lost when love leaks out and living becomes selfish." Involvement in worthy activities that give life purpose and meaning may help to counteract some of the negative effects that retirement has on health, and that is the subject of the next chapter.

CHAPTER 4

The Alternative

*"Vanity is to wish a long life and take but little pains
about a good life."* — *Thomas à Kempis*

I S THERE AN ALTERNATIVE to retiring to a life of leisure, self-absorption, inactivity, and separation from others, leading to boredom and mental and physical decline? Of course there is. The alternative—on which this book is based—is to find a sense of worthy purpose and direction for the retirement years. Maintaining purpose and meaning is so important because it is key to effective adaptation to the stressful life events that typically occur during this period—changes in social roles and status, loss of loved ones through death or relocation, and eventually, the onset of physical illness and disability.[1] I examine here the alternative to an inactive retirement and discuss new sources of purpose in later life, the importance of having a "vision" for one's retirement years, and the need to plan for an active retirement that is productive and fulfilling. I also review medical research that has looked at the effects of having "purpose" on mental and physical health.

MAKING THE BIG DECISION

Wil Rose, cofounder and president of the National Heritage Foundation, once said, "Live each day as though it were your last—for one day you will be right." How many people have a direction, purpose, and goal for the remaining years of life so that every day can be lived as if it were their last? At what target do most retired people aim their arrows of time, talent, and financial resources? Many want to do something in their last years that will give life meaning and leave a mark on the world. Retirement presents opportunities like never before to make a difference in the lives of others that will last far into the future.

There is something better than spending this precious time pursuing recreation and leisure and seeking fulfillment focused on the self—the harder that happiness is sought in those directions, the more quickly it flees. As Nathaniel Hawthorne once said, "Happiness in this world when it comes, comes incidentally. Make it the object of pursuit, and it is never attained." How does happiness come about incidentally in retirement? Part of the answer has to do with having purpose—especially, the right purpose.

This does not mean turning to a life of asceticism and self-deprivation, completely void of pleasure or enjoyment. In fact, the very opposite is true. Recreation and a little self-indulgence are definitely part of the picture. The difference is that they are not at the *center* of the picture, the focus of ultimate concern. More like a dessert than a main course. It is only when our attention and our focus—our purpose—are outside ourselves that pleasure can be fully savored. This pleasure is long lasting, not something that disappears when desperately grasped, as does self-centered pleasure.

🌿 THE IMPORTANCE OF PURPOSE

Phillips Brooks, one of America's greatest preachers during the nineteenth century, said, "Sad will be the day for every man when he becomes contented with the life he is living, and there is no longer some great desire to do something larger which he knows that he was meant and made to do." Purpose is the great desire that helps structure time and resources so we can make progress toward meaningful goals during retirement. Having a purpose helps to motivate and energize people. Purpose helps us establish priorities that are worthwhile and life-enhancing. Purpose provides momentum to overcome the obstacles, challenges, and stressful circumstances that occur with aging. In addition, as people look back during the process of life review, accomplishments and progress toward worthwhile goals will be satisfying and contribute to their sense of integrity. When people have no direction or goals, they wander aimlessly through life, fail to realize their full potential, and sometimes look back with despair over wasted time and opportunities.

The Jewish psychiatrist Victor Frankl, one of the few who survived the horrors of the Nazi concentration camps, emphasized the importance of finding meaning and purpose. He said that it was the key to survival when his choices were few and the future appeared hopeless.[2] He and other camp prisoners who maintained a sense of meaning or purpose in life were the ones able to transcend the dismal surroundings and desperate physical circumstances of the camps and ultimately got through the horrific experience, while those who could not ended up dying. Frankl attributed his own and others' survival to the power of having a sense of purpose that kept their eyes on meaningful goals ahead. Purpose can help us survive retirement as well, and more than just survive, actually live triumphantly as worthy goals are reached and a difference is made in the world.

The purposes of young adulthood or middle age, however, are often not sufficient for the retirement years. With age, wisdom, and experience, people sometimes realize that earlier priorities, values, and goals have been misplaced, shallow, or otherwise less important when looking back from the standpoint of adult maturity. There are also different needs to fulfill in this last life stage, which is characterized by a struggle between "integrity versus despair."[3] This means that old goals will have to be set aside or modified and that new, more substantial and meaningful goals for this last life stage will need to be identified and pursued. Letting go, however, is never easy.

❧ SAYING GOODBYE

Salento (handwritten annotation)

Deciding to have a new purpose for the retirement years requires acceptance of change. Change is inevitable—it comes whether we want it or not—especially with aging. Change can be resisted and fought, or accepted and used to begin something new. Leo Tolstoy said, "Everybody thinks of changing humanity but nobody thinks of changing himself." On the one hand, many people resist change. People crave continuity—to remain the same, to continue with the usual routines. On the other hand, they cannot stand sameness or lack of change. Monotonous routine results in boredom, restlessness, and a desire for something different or new.

Life is all about change—the changing seasons from spring through winter, the changing weather, the changing temperature, the changing position of the sun throughout the day. Change characterizes our interactions with family and friends. It can't be helped. People also enjoy change—they want something different to eat at each meal, different programs and news to watch on television, different stories in the newspaper each day. Humans require change and contrast. If they don't have it, as sensory deprivation experiments have shown, they become stark raving mad. For example, if a person is immersed in water at body temperature and all light and sound are cut off, scientists have found that he will soon begin to hallucinate—his brain will produce change on its own with no outside input. Change is necessary—and yet it is often difficult.

Retirement is a time to say goodbye—goodbye to old sources of purpose and meaning. But how does a person know what to let go of and what to hang on to? What are the characteristics of things to let go of? Some things have to be let go whether you want to or not—for example, the routines of an old job, your identity as worker or boss or supervisor, perhaps your role as instructor, nurturer, and protector of your children as they leave to establish their own families. There are some hard goodbyes that many will have to say, particularly as advanced age sets in. Goodbye to loved ones as they become sick and die, goodbye to friends and neighbors when they move or relocate, goodbye to vigorous health and independence when sickness or disability strike. Remember that the old must end before the new can begin, as fall and winter precede the springtime.

It is important to prioritize among the things you willingly say goodbye to. Deciding on a *purpose* for your retirement years will help you determine what to hold on to and what to let go. Since time and resources are limited, these choices should be made strategically and consciously in line with your purpose. Often this is done unconsciously. Each person has priorities, spoken or unspoken, consciously chosen or unconscious. It is important to take time to consciously choose a worthy purpose for retirement, given the role it will play in setting your future priorities.

❧ SAYING HELLO TO NEW PURPOSE

Retirement (and preferably, well before retirement) is when a new purpose should be chosen. That purpose will then direct your activities and structure your time during this final one-third of life—that may last forty years or more for some. Given the length of time now spent in retirement, it is truly almost enough to start a second life. What an exciting opportunity—to start life over, but to begin this time with all the wisdom and experience gained over the years.

So what are your options? What are the characteristics of

sources of purpose that have potential? In other words, what kinds of goals can be set for retirement that will be energizing, motivating, and enjoyable as one strives toward them? Remember, it's not about arriving, but about the journey. Here are some suggestions.

Choose a purpose that takes advantage of your strengths and abilities.

Choose a purpose that takes into consideration your current strengths, talents, capacities, and resources. For example, a person with poor vision, no flying experience, and on a limited budget would not decide to borrow money to purchase an airplane and then pilot it to make food drops to starving people in Afghanistan. No, that would be silly. First, make a thorough inventory of your talents—your natural abilities, training, and experiences. Second, ask yourself what kind of work you performed when you were employed and what were you particularly good at. Is there an area about which you are especially knowledgeable—medicine, law, business, gardening, or cooking? Do you have a particular skill, like playing a musical instrument, making crafts, doing plumbing, electrical work, or carpentry?

Third, what kind of personality do you have? Extroverts enjoy talking and interacting with people. Introverts are stressed out by people and happiest when carrying out projects alone or with a few close friends. Do you tend to be a leader, organizer, or manager, a take-charge kind of individual, or do you prefer to follow directions and complete specific tasks that are assigned by someone else? Do you take pride in being logical, rational, and able to find solutions to problems? Or do you see your strength in being caring, compassionate, and nourishing, a good listener and encourager? Do you tend to be patient and long-suffering, or alternatively, impatient, easily irritated, and wanting to see results quickly?

Fourth, what do you enjoy doing? What kinds of activities have you enjoyed in the past? What activities give you pleasure, so that you look forward to doing them? What kinds of things have you spent hours and hours doing when time just seemed to fly by? What kinds of activities excite you and energize you, rather than bore you and drain your strength?

Finally, what are your limitations? How is your physical health and endurance? Are you disabled in some way? Do you have difficulty walking and moving about, trouble hearing, problems with vision, or difficulty with coordination? Do you have chronic lung disease or chronic congestive heart failure that limits physical activity? What about financial resources? Are you able to live comfortably on your present income and assets, or do you need to work in order to live from day to day? Do you have sufficient money put away that will last during your retirement years? How much disposable income is there each month? What about time? How much free time is available? Do you have other responsibilities to family members, community organizations, your church, or volunteer groups that need fulfilling?

Choose a purpose that has flexibility.

Goals must be flexible in terms of your future abilities. They should be achievable regardless of the changes you are likely to encounter up ahead. The reality is that older adults experience health problems that limit and restrict them, and they are hard to predict. Financial problems may arise because of hospital bills or other unanticipated expenses. These new restrictions may prompt a modification of goals or at least a change of the pathway to pursuing goals. Purpose, however, need not be affected. Remember that purpose is the motor, the engine that drives us toward our goals. If someone is driving along and encounters a tree across the road on the way to his destination, he will not give up and go back home. Instead, he will get out a map and look for alternative routes to that destination. His car's motor remains unaltered as the power source that will take him over different roads to where he decides to go. The same is true for purpose as it moves a person toward chosen goals. What determines the power in purpose, of course, is the *worthiness* of the goals.

Your purpose should have the potential for significant impact.

Your purpose ought to have some kind of impact in the world; it should make a meaningful difference for at least one other person. If your effort has little impact or if its impact is entirely self-directed, then the worthiness of the goal must be questioned. For example, a person may choose to drive from New York to Los Angeles and back to New York again. The sights would be interesting and new things might be discovered, but if the effects were entirely confined to the person taking the journey, then the journey's potential for impact would be relatively low. The world wouldn't be much different as a result of the trip. If, however, she sought by the trip to affect even one other person in a positive way (or to rejuvenate or educate herself so that she could make an impact after her return), the impact would increase substantially.

Impact need not be defined on a large scale or by the number of people who are affected. Someone might, without expectation of reward, expend a great deal of effort and resources to improve the circumstances of one other person. Such efforts might be associated with considerable impact and could have consequences hard to predict. For example, the single person affected might help someone else, who in turn might help someone else, and so on, until a wave of generosity spreads out as a consequence of the initial deed. The world is often changed through the accumulated effects of many small kindnesses. The following true story illustrates this point.[4]

In the 1890s there was a very important inventor by the name of Whitcomb L. Judson who worked hard to create a revolutionary transportation system for Chicago. This was a huge contribution that placed Judson's name into the history books because of his accomplishment. One day, Judson learned that a father of a friend had severe arthritis in his fingers that made it difficult for him to manipulate the many tiny hooks that held people's clothes and shoes on in those days. The friend asked Judson if there was anything he could design that would make it easier for his father to fasten his shoes than the tiny hooks. Despite the fact that Judson was preoccupied with his enormous transportation project, he chose to take time to help his friend. As Whitcomb tried to figure out a way to keep shoes on easier, he invented a little contraption known as the zipper. During Judson's lifetime, very little attention was paid to the zipper and he didn't sell many of them. After he died, however, the zipper soon became enormously popular, as it remains to this day. When he designed the zipper for his friend's father, Judson had no intention of discovering something that would make him famous and rich—he just wanted to help a man with painful fingers to keep his shoes on. The consequences of that kind act, however, changed the world for the better. Which one of Judson's accomplishments had more impact? It's hard to say.

Albert Einstein said, "Only a life lived for others is a life worthwhile." There are not many actions that have true significance and meaning if no one else is affected. The effects that our actions have on others establish them as worthy. For example, if a person expends a great deal of time and resources climbing a mountain and is successful, while he may experience a feeling of satisfaction and accomplishment, the action affects no one else in a significant way. The action is entirely self-centered. Don't get me wrong—there's nothing wrong with climbing mountains or performing actions that one alone benefits from. In my younger years, I myself was a mountain climber and solitary explorer. However, if your action does not benefit others, either directly or indirectly, then your focus is still solely on yourself. It is important to focus on yourself at times, but if your goal and motive in life is self-fulfillment only, it won't provide you with much purpose.

The altruistic nature of an action is important; in other words, the action is not performed with the sole intention of receiving a reward or having one's own personal needs met. For example, suppose a man decides to perform an act of kindness by visiting a disabled homebound widow in the neighborhood. His intention would be to relieve the widow's loneliness and make her feel loved and cared for. If, however, he makes the visit because it is known that the widow is very wealthy and might provide a handsome reward for such attention, his good action is entirely self-centered. This is an extreme example, but it illustrates the point that for actions to serve a worthy purpose, they must be truly other-directed and not entirely self-directed. Having purpose that gives real power requires a focus on others or at least on another. As Ralph Waldo Emerson said, "The purpose of life is not to be happy. It is to be useful, to be honorable, to be compassionate, to have it make some difference that you have lived and lived well."

Your purpose should have a spiritual aspect.

If your purpose has a spiritual dimension, the power to reach your goals increases enormously. In addition, having a spiritual dimension magnifies the intrinsic rewards as you strive to fulfill that purpose. By spiritual I mean having some connection with God and God's will. Having a spiritual aspect, then, means that actions are in some way performed to further God's purposes. While it may be difficult to determine exactly what God's purposes are, and there are many different understandings of God that might influence that determination, common principles exist that are found in all major religious teachings. Chief among these common principles are to love and care for your neighbor and to attend to the needs of others, in contrast to being focused on your own comfort and pleasures. Western religions also place a particular emphasis on *action*. The universe is constantly moving and changing. To keep up, a person needs to be action-oriented. God has given people free will to determine their destiny. God has given power, dominion, and authority to humans as part of creation. But it is up to us to choose to take action.

🌺 ACTIVITIES THAT FULFILL PURPOSE

Only certain kinds of actions guide a person toward goals that are worthy enough to provide sustained purpose. On the one hand, say someone determines that his goal in retirement is to make as much money as he possibly can so that he can have control and power over others. This may provide great purpose as he takes action to strive toward that goal. Aging, however, usually leads to limits on one's earning capacity and to limited opportunities with regard to gathering wealth. It is likely, then, that the goal to earn a lot of money will be frustrated by one circumstance or another and could quickly lead to disillusionment. Even if our retiree succeeds, given that the goal is entirely self-centered, it is not clear how much fulfillment he will actually experience. On the other hand, say he chooses to seek to improve the lives of others by helping to meet their physical, psychological, social, or spiritual needs, with little expectation of reward. In this case, many activities can be engaged in to achieve the goal and any actions taken are quite likely to succeed and be fulfilling, especially if motives are "right."

So, what kinds of purpose-filled activities can a retired person get involved in? For those needing to draw a small amount of income to make ends meet, who still wish to invest in the lives of others in meaningful ways, there are the Foster Grandparent Program, Senior Opportunities for Services Programs, and Operation Mainstream. These government programs provide earnings at the federal minimum wage. If income is not needed, there are numerous government-sponsored volunteer activities such as the Retired Senior Volunteer Program (RSVP), Peace Corps, Service Corps of Retired Executives (SCORE), Volunteers and Service to America (VISTA), and International Executive Service Corps (IESC). Many other formal and informal kinds of helping and volunteer activities exist that I will discuss further in chapter 5.

❧ PURPOSE WITH PHYSICAL ILLNESS

Physical illness and disability present real challenges. They do so by taking away independence and making inaccessible those things that provided purpose and meaning when we were younger and more able. I know this for a fact, given my personal battle with pain and disability from arthritis for the past twenty years. When your way of life is dramatically changed by illness, it sometimes stimulates a search for new sources of meaning. People with chronic illness are by no means excluded from experiencing purpose and power. One of the great advantages of purpose is that it is not limited by circumstances. In fact, difficult circumstances often represent the fertile soil of opportunity—opportunity for new direction and purpose that can have more impact than ever before. When a person is well and healthy, he or she can be entrapped by goals that have little ultimate meaning or significance. Illness often forces people to reevaluate and shed previous dreams and goals. Failing to redirect purpose and redefine goals in such circumstances can result in depression, despair, and loss of usefulness—and often does.

Rather than being focused on acquiring more possessions, more influence over others, or more self-centered pleasures, being unable to do so any longer because of illness forces attention toward higher, more important goals. The type of illness that one has may contain clues for that new purpose. It is the illness and limitations brought on by illness that can point the way.

For example, a person with arthritis and chronic pain may find that his or her suffering provides insight, compassion, and motivation to help others who also experience pain.[5] Similarly, a woman diagnosed with breast cancer may join a support group to encourage and support other women with breast cancer. A homebound elderly person may decide to relieve loneliness by calling other homebound persons on the telephone and offering support, encouragement, and companionship. A person with chronic depression may decide to reach out to others who are disheartened and without hope, offering companionship that will lessen the burden of suffering.

The physically ill person may also, in desperation, seek spiritual solace. This may involve renewing a relationship with God or with a spiritual community. As a result, he or she may experience a new calling to serve others in some small way, still within his or her ability. For the spiritual person, opportunities for fulfilling God's divine will abound everywhere, especially in circumstances that would otherwise appear dismal. Disabled and dependent people can serve, if only by their attitudes of gratefulness and appreciation for the care they receive from others. The spiritual person can be a missionary to everyone she meets, sharing God's kindness, love, and truth in whatever circumstance arises, and praying for others when physical actions are no longer possible. Those in nursing homes and other institutional settings are no exception. The spiritual person in a nursing home may decide to give the gifts of friendliness and companionship by engaging in conversations with other residents, offering time to listen, and, if needed, supplying encouragement and hope. Serving in this way energizes and empowers the sick, gives them vision and purpose, and, while not guaranteed, may even lead to better physical health for some. As lives take on new meaning and purpose, the body's natural healing

mechanisms may be invigorated (for example, immune function may be boosted).

❧ HEALTH CONSEQUENCES OF PURPOSE

Plenty of scientific research shows the difference having a life's
purpose makes on well-being and health. This is especially true
for research that has examined the relationship between purpose and mental health in later life.

Purpose may be especially important for those recovering
from addictive disorders like alcoholism.[6] Purpose in the setting
of chronic alcoholism has been shown to interact with spiritual practices to increase the length of sobriety. For example,
Stephanie Carroll examined the relationship between spirituality and recovery from alcoholism in a sample of one hundred
alcoholics participating in Alcoholics Anonymous.[7] In that
study, spirituality was defined as the extent to which the subject
practiced Step 11—involving prayer and meditation—of the
twelve-step program. The investigator found significant positive correlations between the practice of Step 11, "purpose in
life" scores, and length of sobriety. Greater purpose in life was
also associated with more Alcoholics Anonymous meetings
attended, which was in turn associated with greater length of
sobriety. The author concluded that a sense of purpose in life is
associated with higher scores on spiritual activities like prayer
and meditation, and that these together may assist in the maintenance of longer sobriety.

Having purpose in life influences the risk of experiencing
depression, regardless of age. For example, Lisa Harlow and colleagues examined the relationship between purpose in life,
negative emotions, and substance abuse in a sample of 722 adolescents.[8] They found that purpose and meaning in life helped
to block the vicious cycle of self-derogation, depression, substance abuse, and suicidal ideation in this population.

British investigators examined the relationship between purpose in life and both positive and negative measures of psychological well-being.[9] They found a strong association between purpose, meaning in life, and well-being, which they were able to replicate in two different samples of people. Purpose in life was found to be more strongly related to positive well-being than to indicators of negative mental health. This finding suggests that having purpose in life may be particularly important in bringing about positive emotions like joy and happiness, rather than simply protecting from negative ones like depression or anxiety.

Not surprisingly, activities like volunteering are especially associated with greater purpose and well-being after retirement. In a study of forty retirees, those who volunteered more than ten hours a week scored significantly higher on a "purpose in life" test than did those who volunteered ten or fewer hours per week. In that study, a significant negative correlation was found between degree of purpose in life and proneness to boredom.[10] Having a sense of purpose also predicts less worry about death and dying among older adults.[11] This may have to do with the impact that purpose in life has on their sense of personal control and autonomy.

As noted earlier, having a sense of meaning and purpose is especially important in the setting of medical illness. Carol McWilliam and colleagues explored factors other than medical ones that influenced the discharge experiences of twenty-one medical patients.[12] Included in the study were 22 informal caregivers and 117 professionals involved in their care. Investigators found that lack of purpose in life contributed to a disempowering process. Even in the face of threats to independence imposed by a biomedically oriented paternalistic health care system, patients with a sense of direction and purpose in life were less likely to experience a threat to autonomy. Researchers concluded that future attention should be placed on empowering patients with a sense of purpose and meaning to help maintain autonomy in the face of the threats imposed by illness and treatment settings.

In another study of medical patients, E. J. Taylor examined factors associated with meaning and progress among seventy-four persons with recurrent cancer.[13] She found significant negative correlations between sense of purpose and symptom distress, social dependency, and length of time since diagnosis of recurrence. Adjustment to illness was clearly associated with greater purpose and meaning. She concluded that a sense of purpose was integrally related to the physical and psychosocial consequences of metastatic cancer, and that health professionals should seek to enhance the patient's sense of purpose and meaning.

Not only is purpose associated with better mental health, then, but as the above study implies, it may also be associated with better physical health. Note that having strong purpose was associated with a longer time since diagnosis of recurrence, suggesting that purpose may have delayed the recurrence of the cancer. Consider also the work of Karen Hooker and Ilene Siegler, who examined the relationship between having life goals (i.e., purpose in life) and perceptions of physical health and vigor.[14] These investigators found that individuals who reported greater achievement of life goals perceived their health as substantially better than those who reported less fulfillment of purpose. Similarly, a study by A. Grand and colleagues found that purpose (feeling useful and having many projects to accomplish) predicted better physical health and vigor regardless of age.[15] In a study of three hundred persons at five developmental stages from young adulthood to the old-old, George Reker and colleagues found that purpose in life increased with increasing age and predicted greater psychological and physical well-being.[16]

There is also evidence that having purpose predicts a longer life span.[17] In one study, investigators followed 6,274 subjects for three years. During the three years, 449 people died. Among the 3,891 women in the study, predictors of survival were younger age, less disability, fewer memory problems, regular health examinations, and greater purpose in life. Thus, purpose in life was an independent predictor of longevity, regardless of age or level of physical disability.

Having a sense of purpose and meaning may also influence the health and well-being of family members who care for sick loved ones.[18] In one study, researchers examined the effect of having purpose on spouse caregiver health.[19] Studying sixty-five spouse caregivers of persons with advanced cancer, they found that sense of purpose was a significant predictor of better caregiver health status. Thus, it appears that those who have strong purpose in life can endure even the most difficult of circumstances and survive—both mentally and physically.

❧ CONCLUSION

There is an alternative to retiring to a life of self-absorption, leisure, and inactivity. That alternative involves identifying a new and higher purpose that can give life meaning and significance, while at the same time accepting the changes associated with advancing age and retirement. Only certain kinds of purpose have the potential to be empowering, so being deliberate about choosing the right goals is essential. Empowering sources of purpose are especially important for persons with acute or chronic medical illness and for loved ones who provide care for them. Having purpose and meaning in life is associated with better mental health, better physical health, and greater longevity. Purpose, then, adds not only years to life, but life to years.

CHAPTER 5

Volunteer

"Volunteerism is what makes the world go 'round."
—James Trammell III

As suggested in the last chapter, volunteering is one way to acquire purpose and power in retirement. It also benefits the community and the nation. In an article entitled "Bowling Alone," Robert Putnam notes that the extent to which people are active in secondary groups such as volunteer associations is a crucial test of the health of civil society.[1] He connects this with the amount of "social capital" that a society possesses. According to Putnam, social capital refers to "those features of social organizations such as networks, norms, and social trust that facilitate coordination and cooperation for mutual benefit."[2]

Social capital declines as people become more private and preoccupied with their own needs. As social capital declines, civic engagement in general and volunteering in particular tend to decline as people put their own narrow interests first and feel disconnected from others in their community. Degree of volunteerism, then, is a key indicator of the health of American society, and retired persons can serve a vital role in maintaining that health. As Herbert Hoover said, "A voluntary deed by a man impressed with a sense of responsibility and brotherhood of man is infinitely precious to our national ideals and spirit."

Many treasured natural resources in this country are declining—oil and precious metals are becoming more scarce; forest lands are shrinking; pristine lakes and unpolluted streams, fresh and uncontaminated air, game and wildlife are all slowly becoming less plentiful. The only natural resource increasing in America is the untapped human resource found in the aging population. With more and more Americans retiring at younger and younger ages, retirees are increasing dramatically in number. By the year 2030, 40 percent of the adult U.S. population aged eighteen or older will be over age fifty-five.[3] Retired persons have at least five key resources that are vital for society: time, experience, civic-mindedness, social capital, and awareness.[4]

Time. Retired persons have time to care. A study done at the University of Maryland found that retirement frees up eighteen to twenty-five hours a week.[5]

Experience. Having lived in the world for over half a century, struggling to overcome family and work problems, retired persons have often gained a great deal of practical knowledge and wisdom about how to approach difficult situations.

Civic-mindedness. Older adults are more concerned about what is going on in municipal, state, and federal governments, as is evidenced by the fact that more persons over age sixty-five vote than any other age group. In 1986, 1990, 1994, and 1998, over 60 percent of persons sixty-five or older voted in congressional elections, compared to 54–59 percent of those forty-five to sixty-four years old, 35–41 percent of those twenty-five to forty-four years old, and 17–22 percent of those eighteen to twenty-four years old.[6]

Social Capital. Retired persons are a key source of social capital, with firsthand knowledge of social and national history that is not available to many young persons. This plays an important role in preserving social norms, as well as in preserving social relationships in the community that have been forged over many years in the face of common struggles.

Awareness. Older adults are more aware of their need to contribute something meaningful to society, since this is a primary psychological need of this life stage (achieving integrity over despair, according to psychologist Eric Erickson).[7] This awareness, often not present among the young, serves as a motivating and energizing force to propel elders to help others in need.

These resources amply equip the retired person to be an excellent volunteer. And as suggested in the last chapter, one of the most effective ways of achieving strong purpose in retirement is to consciously set aside time to use your resources to make life better for others. A truth is a truth—one that keeps coming back around over and over again. Consider what has been said about helping others:

> "Dear friends, let us love one another, for love comes from God." —1 John 4:7

> "Above all, love each other deeply." —1 Peter 4:8

> "To me it seems that to give happiness is a far nobler goal than to attain it: and that what we exist for is much more a matter of relations to others than a matter of individual progress: much more a matter of helping others to heaven than of getting there ourselves." —Lewis Carroll (British author and mathematician)

> "A strong nation, like a strong person, can afford to be gentle, firm, thoughtful, and restrained. It can afford to extend a helping hand to others. It's a weak nation, like a weak person, that must behave with bluster and boasting and rashness and other signs of insecurity." —Jimmy Carter

"The basis of world peace is the teaching which runs through almost all the great religions of the world. 'Love thy neighbor as thyself.' Christ, some of the other great Jewish teachers, Buddha, all preached it. Their followers forgot it. What is the trouble between capital and labor, what is the trouble in many of our communities, but rather a universal forgetting that this teaching is one of our first obligations." —Eleanor Roosevelt

"The poor don't know that their function in life is to exercise our generosity." —Jean-Paul Sartre

"The act of neighbor helping neighbor has been one of the distinguishing marks of America and one of the primary causes of our nation's greatness." —Ronald Reagan

"From now on in America the true measure of success will have to reflect man's commitment to his community." —George W. Bush

❧ DEFINITION

Volunteering is an activity whereby people set aside time to provide companionship to the lonely, tutoring to the illiterate, counseling to the troubled, health care to the sick, or many other formal and informal services on a regular, ongoing basis without charge and without being forced to do so. Volunteering is a form of "planned helping" that consists of sorting out priorities and matching personal interests and abilities to the needs of others. Volunteers must decide on how much time to set aside for such activity, how involved to become, and to what extent the activity meets their own needs. Volunteering may involve *seeking out* opportunities to help others. It always requires commitment to a helping relationship that may extend over time and entail a considerable amount of time, energy, and other personal resources. It is not usually a spontaneous, spur-of-the-moment behavior, and so should not be confused with "good Samaritan acts"—quick responses that are quickly over. The latter, however, are also important; as Benjamin Franklin said, "Always be ready to serve any other person that may need your assistance." This, however, is not the same as deciding to become a volunteer.

Volunteering must also be distinguished from simple social participation. Much social participation is largely expressive (involvement in a sports club, for example) or self-interested (involvement in a labor union). However, some social participation involves contributing time for the benefit of the needy or for the prevention of community problems. Volunteer work of this kind is a lot more demanding and self-sacrificing than mere participation in a voluntary association. How common, then, is volunteering?

❧ VOLUNTEERING IN THE UNITED STATES

Volunteering is found throughout the world.[8] This section, however, will focus on the United States. In 1998, 56 percent of Americans volunteered (109 million persons), contributing 20 billion hours of service.[9] The value of this volunteer time was estimated at $226 billion (excluding informal volunteering). Of Americans who attended religious services weekly or more often, nearly three-quarters (72.6 percent) volunteered. What do people volunteer for? Approximately 24 percent of volunteering involves providing informal services to those in need; 22 percent volunteer for religious organizations; 18 percent volunteer for youth development; 17 percent in schools for education; 16 percent in human services organizations; 11 percent in health areas; 10 percent in work-related organizations; 9 percent in environmental programs; 9 percent in arts, culture, and humanities; and 9 percent in recreation (coaching, refereeing).

The rate of volunteering, however, is decreasing. Between

1991 and 1995, Americans who volunteered spent an average of 4.2 hours a week in this activity, compared to 3.5 hours a week in 1998.[10] Although weekly church attendees volunteered more time each week than did the average American (4.0 hours a week versus 3.5 hours), even that figure is down from 4.8 hours a week in 1989. For persons attending religious services less often than weekly, the average amount of time spent volunteering was 3.2 hours a week in 1998.

In his book *Prime Time*, Marc Freedman notes that part of the reason for the decline in volunteering is that 62 percent of mothers with preschoolers and 50 percent of all mothers with infants are now working at paid jobs. Back in 1960, the percentage of mothers with preschoolers who worked in paid jobs was only 19 percent. With women moving into the workforce, it is not surprising that PTA membership has dropped dramatically. In the mid-1960s, there were 12 million PTA members. Today there are only 7 million, despite an increase in the population since that time.[11]

Changes in public policy are also shifting more and more of the responsibility for tackling social problems away from government and onto nonprofit agencies and religious organizations (who depend heavily on volunteers to accomplish their goals). This increase in demand for volunteer labor comes at a time when more and more people are working longer hours (to maintain the American standard of living) and have less free time for leisure and volunteering.[12]

❧ VOLUNTEERING DURING RETIREMENT

Even when time begins to free up, as it does in retirement, volunteering does not increase. According to gerontologists John Rowe and Robert Kahn, fewer than one-third of all older persons volunteer, and even those who do so spend less than two hours a week in this activity.[13] Recent figures are somewhat more promising, but still underscore the point. While 56 percent of Americans did some volunteer work, only 48 percent of persons over fifty-five did so.[14] Older Americans also spent less time volunteering than younger persons. While persons of all ages volunteered an average of 3.5 hours a week doing volunteer work, persons over fifty-five volunteered an average of 3.3 hours a week—or less than 10 percent of their available leisure time. Among those fifty-five to sixty-four, 50 percent volunteer (averaging 3.3 hours a week); of those sixty-five to seventy-four, 47 percent volunteer (averaging 3.6 hours a week); and among those seventy-five or over, 43 percent volunteer (averaging 3.1 hours per week). Retired persons are more likely to volunteer for religious organizations (26 percent) and provide informal helping (18 percent), rather than volunteering for youth programs (8 percent), human services (8 percent), education (6 percent), art and culture (6 percent), public benefit (4 percent), or in health areas (3 percent).

Thus, despite the fact that retired persons have more time to volunteer and help others, they are less likely to do so. Even when health and financial resources are taken into account, there is no evidence that people are more likely to volunteer when they retire. For example, note that the young elderly aged fifty-five to sixty-four (typically in good health) also volunteer less than persons in middle age who have families to raise and are at the peak of their professional careers.[15]

🌿 WHO VOLUNTEERS?

Studies have examined the characteristics of persons who volunteer. Educated people are significantly more likely to volunteer than those with less education.[16] At least in part, education increases the likelihood of volunteering by increasing awareness of community problems and by enhancing a sense of civic responsibility. To what extent does gender influence volunteering, since the general impression is that women volunteer more than men? Overall, there are no gender differences in volunteering—men are as likely to volunteer as women.[17] Volunteering peaks in middle age, and the average volunteer tends to be married and have children living in the household. Persons with higher status and more social connections are more likely to volunteer and to be asked to volunteer. Volunteers also tend to rate their health better and complain less often about physical disability.[18]

Religion is a major factor in volunteering, and volunteers are much more likely to have strong moral values about helping those who suffer. Nearly 70 percent of all volunteering among older adults is done within a religious setting, and those who attend religious services are most likely to volunteer.[19] One-third of those who do not belong to a religious organization volunteer, compared to more than 60 percent of church members. In a study of over 1,700 churchgoing Protestants, the strongest predictors of volunteering were religiosity, religious identity, religious socialization, and especially, level of involvement in church activities.[20]

The type of work that people do while in the workforce also predicts their likelihood of volunteering. John Wilson and Marc Musick surveyed 1,502 full-time employed persons in 1986 and interviewed them again in 1989 as part of the Americans' Changing Lives survey.[21] Half the sample volunteered in one or more groups, most commonly in religious activity (28 percent), with education (21 percent) next. Professionals employed by business corporations were the most likely of all professionals to volunteer. The largest *number* of volunteer activities was reported by self-employed sales and clerical workers, such as insurance agents, independent realtors, freelance designers, computer programmers, or stock and bond salespeople (white-collar workers). Next most likely to volunteer were managers. Managers, in turn, were more likely to volunteer than blue-collar workers.

Private sector blue-collar workers were the least likely to volunteer.

Researchers speculated that the reason for this pattern was that private sector blue-collar workers' jobs afford them less autonomy and self-direction, which are strong predictors of volunteering. On the other hand, higher status workers such as professionals and managers not only have more autonomy and self-direction, but also bring more personal resources to volunteer work and are more likely to be socially active as part of their jobs (since managers are often expected to involve themselves in community affairs).

Those who work in *public* sector jobs also tend to volunteer more than others. On average, public sector workers put in 3.6 hours of volunteer work a week, compared to 2.9 hours for self-employed workers and 1.9 hours for private sector workers. Why is this so? According to experts, public sector workers are more likely to see their jobs as a "calling," are more likely to integrate their work and social lives more smoothly, and are more exposed to community problems and needs.

Race also makes a difference in volunteering. Whites tend to volunteer more than blacks, although there are interesting reasons for this pattern. Musick and his colleagues examined the effects of race and social class on volunteering among a random sample of 2,867 Americans.[22] The mean number of hours volunteered by whites was about 50 percent greater than for blacks. They discovered that while whites are better endowed with education, financial resources, and technical skills (human social capital), blacks have more social and cultural resources that partially compensate for a lack of other resources. They also found that blacks are less likely to be asked to volunteer than whites and are also less likely to accept a volunteer invitation if made.

Volunteering among blacks is more influenced by religion than it is among whites, a consequence of the major role the church plays in the black community. A 1989 Independent

Sector survey found that blacks were more likely than whites to volunteer for church-related activities—but also for community-action groups, work-related organizations, and political groups. Whites were more likely to volunteer in areas related to youth, education, the environment, and the arts. Even among black church attendees, however, degree of religiosity is a strong predictor of volunteer behaviors. Musick and colleagues found that among blacks attending church once a week or more, strong believers were twice as likely to volunteer than weak believers (47 percent to 23 percent). At least one study has found that blacks are more likely than whites to indicate altruistic motives for volunteering. Whereas whites are more likely to say that they volunteered because "it seemed like an opportunity to learn new things," blacks are more likely to say, "I believed it was my duty to help contribute to the community."[23]

❧ WHY VOLUNTEER?

In general, then, why do people volunteer? What kinds of things factor into this important decision? Interestingly, only about one out of five volunteers "seeks out" volunteering on his or her own. According to volunteer expert Doug Lawson, most people first start volunteering after they are asked by others to do so or are assigned to a task. The following are common reasons given for volunteering:[24]

+ Want to carry on the traditions of their families.
+ Are asked to volunteer by relatives, friends, or members of their community.
+ Believe that their efforts will benefit others.
+ Want *to do something useful and meaningful* (two-thirds of respondents).

Social psychologist Gil Clary and his colleagues have tried to understand the reasons for volunteering in terms of personal motivations.[25] They understand volunteering as serving six functions: values, understanding, social, career, protective, and enhancement.

Values. People volunteer in order to express values of altruistic and humanitarian concern for others. This is a way for people to express deeply held beliefs, dispositions, and convictions.

Understanding. Volunteering permits new learning experiences and chances to exercise knowledge, skills, and abilities.

Social. Social motivations for volunteering include having more opportunities to be with friends and engage in activities that are viewed favorably by others. Volunteering may help people fit in better with important reference groups and thereby improve their social adjustment.

Career. Career motivations may include volunteering to prepare for a new career or to maintain career-relevant skills, such as business or health care.

Protective. Protective motivations have to do with activity designed to reduce guilt over being more fortunate than others or to reduce negative feelings such as depression or boredom.

Enhancement. The enhancement function of volunteering enables people to enhance their well-being, personal growth, and self-esteem.

Clary and his colleagues developed the Volunteer Functions Inventory (VFI) to assess more carefully these six functions of volunteering. They found that volunteers who score higher on each of the six dimensions of the VFI find volunteer activities more satisfying (especially those who score high on values and enhancement functions). Individuals who perceive their initial motivations as being satisfied through volunteering are more likely to volunteer in the immediate future. Subjects who are high in motivation to volunteer and who receive relevant benefits are also more likely to indicate that they would be active as volunteers as far as five years into the future. Thus, not only are volunteers who score high on the VFI more satisfied with their volunteer activities, they are also more likely to continue them both in the short and the long term. Investigators stress, however, that service opportunities must match initial motivations.

Are some reasons for volunteering better than others? Good reasons might include: seeing a need that resonates with past experiences, wanting to do something significant that gives life meaning, wanting to carry on a family tradition, having religious grounds for volunteering, or volunteering because it is the right thing to do. Fairly good reasons for volunteering might include responding to someone who asks you to volunteer or having extra time on your hands, needing something to do to keep from getting bored, or wanting to learn new things. Not so good reasons for volunteering include feeling guilty because others are doing it or volunteering in order to obtain appreciation or payback from others. An old Chinese proverb says it plainly: "When helping others, do not look for a reward; if you are looking for rewards, don't help others."

❧ STAGES OF VOLUNTEERING

It is helpful to understand the various emotions that people experience over time as they volunteer. In his book *More Give to Live*, Doug Lawson describes three stages of volunteering that focus on emotional and cognitive experiences.[26] The first stage he calls the "helper's high."

Stage 1. In February 1987, the magazine *Better Homes and Gardens* included a brief article about helping others and asked readers to write in about their own helping experiences and how it made them feel. A total of 246 readers sent letters back in response. Immediately after starting to help others, 68 percent of respondents indicated experiencing a distinct physical sensation while they were helping. About 50 percent reported that they experienced a "high" feeling, 43 percent felt stronger and more energetic, 28 percent felt warmer, 22 percent felt calmer and less depressed, 21 percent experienced greater self-worth, and 13 percent experienced fewer aches and pains. Responders who exercised regularly pointed out some similarities between this feeling and the feeling they got after a vigorous physical workout such as swimming, running, or tennis. Although the physiological changes that occur in the body during the process of helping others have not yet been scientifically measured, there is evidence that certain chemicals in the brain called "endorphins" (the body's natural opiates or mood enhancers) have the capacity to stimulate feelings similar to the highs reported by these women.

George Stefano and his colleagues have described new research detailing how a chemical called nitric oxide can induce feelings of warmth, peace, and relaxation.[27] They hypothesize that this chemical is released throughout the body during deep relaxation and whenever one experiences a general feeling of warmth, such as during a special time with loved ones, during times of religious worship or group singing, and during prayer and other spiritual experiences. The release of nitric oxide may indeed cause the feeling of warmth that those in the magazine survey described as occurring when they were helping others. Scientists are just beginning to learn about the positive consequences of nitric oxide release, and they could be quite significant—affecting the immune system, the heart, and blood pressure.

If endorphins and nitric oxide increase when doing good for others or showing compassion and kindness, then selfishness and self-preoccupation may cut off the flow of these chemicals and instead initiate a fight-flight response—with increasing release of adrenaline and steroid hormones that have proven negative health consequences (see chapter 8).

Stage 2. The emotional experiences in the second stage of volunteering occur over time as one continues to help and it becomes a habit.[28] During this stage, a longer lasting sense of satisfaction and emotional warmth emerges that returns with each memory of the event—even long after the helping act has been completed. In the magazine survey discussed above, 80 percent of respondents indicated that the "glow" of helping returned when the helping act was remembered, although it lost intensity as time elapsed since the helping event.

Stage 3. Psychological changes during the third stage of volunteering are associated with long-term changes in personality and feelings about the self. An individual begins to feel stronger and better about the kind of person he or she has become, which leads to greater self-acceptance and a deep sense of inner happiness. Finally, over time, as the volunteer behavior becomes frequent and more consistent, the emotional consequences become more widespread as relationships form with those helped and with others on the helping team. As noted above, the emotional changes associated with volunteering are likely to have physiological consequences that medical researchers are only now beginning to understand.

❧ SUCCESSFUL VOLUNTEERING

What are some keys to successful volunteering? Lawson suggests the following. First, provide services to one person at a time, making one-on-one direct contact. This in-person interaction is essential to obtaining the full benefits of volunteering. Mother Teresa said, "Our work brings people face-to-face with love. To us what matters is an individual. To get to love the person we must have close contact with him." When asked about her secret to getting volunteers, Mother Teresa said: "I just ask them to come and love the people, to give their hands to serve them and their hearts to love them."

Second, the person being helped should be a stranger. Of course, this does not mean you should neglect the needs of family and friends. However, there is something about helping a total stranger who is incapable of reciprocating the good deed that evokes special feelings of reward.

Third, don't expect a specific outcome. Simply find out what the needs are and meet those needs in a sensitive and kind manner, allowing the situation to evolve naturally over time. The situation may take a completely different turn from what you might have expected, but simply ride it out and look for good things to come out of it. The outcome of self-sacrificing acts and kindness needs to be left in the hands of the Creator, and any attempts to control it are likely to fail.

Fourth, every volunteer should be prepared to perform activities that at times will be intense and demanding. During the holidays, some colleagues and I deliver meals to needy people in the community. My job is the task of driving and finding the houses where meals are to be delivered. These are often times when I can feel my blood pressure rise, along with the blood pressure of those who ride with me, as we're getting lost and getting on each other's nerves. This is all part of the price of combating the pervasive evil of deprivation and need. The reward may or may not be immediate but only discovered over time— or perhaps may never be discovered in this life at all, but only in the next.

The return on such investments of time and effort, however,

is vast and probably immeasurable. In my own life, I see the effects on my children, on my friends who help out, on our relationships, even on the relationships between those who are helped and others in their community (in terms of race relations). Lawson reminds us, however, that if volunteering is done for the wrong reason or in the wrong way, these tremendous rewards will not be realized and burnout can rapidly occur—especially when dealing with difficult cases.

❧ MENTAL HEALTH CONSEQUENCES

Can happiness and contentment be bought? It's what most people try to do these days, and it doesn't seem that they are getting much for their money. Maybe there is a better way. A good deed is called a "mitzvah" in the Jewish Torah, which indicates that selfless acts have multiple consequences—they connect a person to God, increase righteousness in the world, decrease alienation and evil, enhance self-esteem, and make everyone much richer and happier.[29] One reason why self-help groups such as Alcoholics Anonymous have been so successful is that they emphasize the need for members to provide companionship and to help support one another. That kind of support is essential for recovery in persons whose lives have been devastated by addiction and who have become isolated from others.

Research suggests that volunteering is indeed associated with better mental health, increased levels of life satisfaction and self-esteem, greater social networks, and more altruistic behavior.[30] Volunteering has been shown to be a source of enhanced career development; it also affects life-career roles and personal identity during the transition from being employed to being retired.[31]

L. I. Wasserbauer and her colleagues in the nursing field suggest that a growing population of educated and skilled younger retirees possess talents to provide volunteer services to the frail elderly in homes, hospitals, and other settings.[32] Such services have the potential to increase the availability of health care services at a time of increasing economic challenges to the health care system. They also enhance the well-being and sense of purpose of these young retired professionals.

Volunteering has been shown to increase the development of life skills and thereby increase autonomy in later life.[33] A study in Italy and the United Kingdom examined factors contributing to the maintenance of autonomy among older persons. Life skills were defined as the development of a positive self-image, feeling at ease in social settings, and having a sense of belonging. Many of the older adults in the study experienced volunteering as key to their development of life skills, to their sense of being independent, and to feeling they were in control of their destinies.

Other investigators point to volumes of research in the social science literature showing that helping others is associated with "improved morale, self-esteem, positive affect, and well-being."[34] According to psychiatrist George Vaillant, who has studied the lives of Harvard graduates over forty years, altruism was one of the few activities that helped even the most poorly adjusted men to overcome stress and to improve their life situations.[35]

Neal Krause and his colleagues examined whether volunteering support to others, especially *informal* kinds of support, results in greater well-being among older adults. Informal kinds of support include providing transportation, shopping assistance, or running errands for friends or neighbors; helping others with housework or upkeep on their house or car; caring for children without pay (besides relatives); and doing other things to help neighbors or friends. In a random national survey of 1,551 Americans whose average age was seventy, Krause and colleagues found that 47 percent provided transportation, shopping, or ran errands for friends or neighbors; 23 percent did housework or home maintenance for others; 25 percent provided child care for friends or neighbors; and 44 percent provided other kinds of tangible support to those not living with them.[36] They found that older adults involved in such informal kinds of support experienced a greater sense of personal control, less depression, and greater well-being.

❧ PHYSICAL HEALTH CONSEQUENCES

No doubt the relationship between health and volunteering is likely to be a complex one. While volunteering is often related to better physical health and greater well-being, it may be that good health and greater sociability lead to more volunteering. Both of these factors may also work together, with better health enabling a person to volunteer and volunteering serving to maintain that good health.

In her book *Abkhasians: The Long-Living People of the Caucasus*, Sula Benet reports on research with this remote population group that lives in the Russian Caucasus region.[37] These are the people who supposedly live an average age of 120 to 150 years. According to her study, the keys to long life reported by the subjects Benet interviewed had to do with their devout religious beliefs and their sense of extended family that included others in the community outside of biological relatives. These people reported feeling obligated to help those who were poor and needy, a practice that was taught and modeled for them by family members. Older adults in the society are highly respected, and everyone attempts to ensure their safety and comfort. There also appears to be less interest in acquiring material possessions and in competing with others, and more interest in providing mutual aid and assistance. There are remarkable parallels here between these subjective reports and studies that have found greater longevity among those who volunteer.

University of California at Berkeley scientists Doug Oman and colleagues studied 1,973 residents ages fifty-five or older living in Marin County, California.[38] Subjects were followed from

1990 through 1995. Thirty-one percent (n = 630) participated in some kind of volunteer activity, and about half of these subjects volunteered for more than one organization. Those who volunteered for two or more organizations experienced a 63 percent lower likelihood of dying during the study period than did non-volunteers. After taking into account the subjects' age, gender, number of chronic conditions, physical mobility, exercise, self-rated general health, health habits (smoking), social support (marital status, religious attendance), and psychological status (depressive symptoms), the size of the effect dropped to 44 percent—still a highly significant difference. The researchers also found that *any level* of volunteering reduced mortality by 60 percent among those who attended religious services weekly. The same was true for participating in other religious group activities and, to a lesser degree, for those who felt "socially connected" and for those involved in *fewer* social activities. Investigators concluded that the positive effects of volunteerism on mortality appear to be particularly strong for those who are more religiously involved.

Volunteering's effects on health have been found in other cultures as well. Neal Krause and his colleagues at the University of Michigan surveyed 2,153 older adults in Japan, examining the relationship between religion, providing help to others, and health.[39] They found that greater religious involvement was associated with providing help to others more often, especially among men. Also, those who provided more assistance to others were significantly more likely to indicate that their physical health was better. The authors concluded that the relationship between religion and better health might have been at least partly explained by the increased likelihood of religious persons helping others.

In conclusion, there appears to be a connection between volunteering and better mental and physical health. There is no definitive proof yet that volunteering results in better health, since the ability to volunteer may be affected by a person's health. Nevertheless, there is ample circumstantial evidence and solid logic to support the idea that those who provide help to others are likely to find that it increases their well-being and health in many ways.

❧ HOW TO GET STARTED

How, then, should a person get started with volunteering? Walter L. Hays said, "Opportunity doesn't knock at the door; she answers when you knock." First, look around. Are there any needs that exist in your community? Does everyone have enough food to eat, a safe place to live? Is everyone financially secure and without worries? Is everyone healthy and independent, and living with those who are also healthy and independent? Does everyone have friends to confide in and receive support from, and is no one feeling lonely or isolated? Are there no children or teenagers who need mentoring? Are the hospitals, nursing homes, orphanages, prisons, and mental institutions in the community closed and without residents? If the answer to all of these questions is yes, then no opportunities for volunteering exist. However, such a community probably does not exist anywhere on the planet Earth. If the answer to any of these questions is no, then your decision to volunteer will likely meet important needs. Start knocking on that door of opportunity.

After looking around and identifying needs, the second step for the prospective volunteer is to examine his or her talents, skills, and resources, and then match them up with a need that exists. This matching process is necessary because volunteering should not be seen as a one-time event but rather as a new pattern of living, involving a long-term commitment of time and energy. John Dewey, one of the most influential thinkers on education in the twentieth century, said, "To find out what one is fitted to do and to secure an opportunity to do it is the key to happiness." When people are using their natural gifts and talents, they are almost always happier and more content. Using those talents for a worthy cause can greatly magnify that happiness and contentment. A chief financial officer of a large corporation might ultimately become bored serving meals to the homeless at a soup kitchen. Put that person's skills to work managing the financial or fundraising operations of the soup kitchen, however, and everyone will benefit.

Third, as suggested in the last chapter on choosing a worthy purpose, prospective volunteers should ask themselves what kinds of activities they have enjoyed in the past. Do they have any hobbies that could be utilized to serve a human need in the community? For example, a man may have a hobby of woodworking that could be utilized to make toys for poor children at Christmas or to make furniture for needy families. A woman who enjoys crocheting or other kinds of crafts may decide to make something and donate it to a local hospital, mission, or other good cause. These are examples of informal kinds of volunteer and helping behaviors that almost anyone can get involved in and have been shown to correlate with well-being and a sense of personal control in later life.

In his book *Why Survive?* Robert Butler lists the more formal types of volunteer activities that retired persons might become involved in:[40] teaching (assisting teachers, tutoring, marking papers, working with children on problem areas, handling recesses, or conducting special courses); history (recording memoirs and assisting in preservation of historical objects for the community); counseling and mentoring youth or those with emotional problems or spiritual struggles; or serving in judicial or administrative roles.

Churches and synagogues are often involved in performing social services for both members of their own congregations and for those in the community. Church-related activities that a retired person may decide to get involved in might include:[41] 1) organizing and carrying out religious services, religious instruction, counseling, choir, music and theater activities; 2) hospital visitation; 3) teen guidance and job counseling for adults, marital counseling, advising on housing or legal assistance; 4) providing meals for seniors or needy families or individuals; 5) providing recreation for elders and young adults, putting on summer camps for young people, coordinating daycare facilities for children; 6) training volunteers for service ministries, running self-help or recovery groups (AA, etc.); 7) providing food and shelter for the homeless, putting on rummage sales for fundraising, helping out families with sick members; and 8) mission activities in and outside of the local community. There are many opportunities to volunteer—the key is identifying the right opportunity that will meet a human need and utilize the individual volunteer's skills and abilities.

❧ INSTITUTIONAL BARRIERS TO VOLUNTEERING

Besides overcoming personal reasons for not volunteering or volunteering for the wrong reason, a person may need to overcome institutional barriers as well. For example, those who volunteer in religious organizations sometimes run into the following problems.[42] Most jobs in churches, synagogues, or temples are not clearly defined, leaving the volunteer uncertain about what is expected. Job descriptions are almost never available, and for that reason structure is often lacking. Not enough time is taken to match talents and gifts to the particular volunteer need. The jobs to be filled may receive more attention than the people filling them—churches often recruit on the basis of "taking turns" rather than sharing gifts. Finally, it is difficult for many people to describe what they're good at, what they're tired of doing, what they don't like to do, what they want to learn, where they are being led to grow, and when they need to take a break from volunteer activities. Religious organizations should invest resources in identifying needs, mobilizing volunteers, and fitting the needs that exist with the talents and preferences of volunteers.

❧ ONLY THE HEALTHY?

Does a person ever get too old to volunteer? Aches and pains, difficulties getting around, or lack of energy may impair a person's ability to volunteer. Can only the healthy and fit volunteer?

Consider the results of a recent study published in the prestigious medical journal *Arthritis & Rheumatism.*[43] Arthritis—with its disabling pain and physical limitations—is a major public health problem among retired persons. Any intervention that could increase the independence and assertiveness of those with arthritis could have enormous impact on the quality of life for millions. One possibility might be to recruit people with arthritis to serve as volunteer lay leaders to help others manage their arthritis. This is similar to the Alcoholics Anonymous approach, which depends on former alcoholics helping and supporting those with current alcohol problems. That's what health psychologists Jenny Hainsworth and Julie Barlow thought, so they designed a study to examine this question and published their results in an article entitled "Volunteers' Experiences of Becoming Arthritis Self-management Lay Leaders: 'It's almost as if I've stopped aging and started to get younger!'"

These investigators wanted to know whether training arthritis patients to become lay leaders who conduct arthritis self-management courses might be associated with improvements in physical and psychological health, self-efficacy (a sense that one is in charge of one's life), use of self-management techniques, and visits to the general practitioner. Twenty-one adults with either osteoarthritis or rheumatoid arthritis (median age of fifty-eight, median disease duration of ten years) were recruited into the study. Subjects were assessed at three points in time: before training to become a lay leader in arthritis self-management, six weeks after training, and six months after training.

The results were remarkable. Six months after training, participants reported significant improvements in arthritis pain, in cognitive symptom management, and in communication with their physicians, as well as significant decreases in depressed mood. Even more important, participants reported having more confidence, greater happiness, even a changed outlook on life in general. The authors concluded that their findings supported the value of volunteerism and training to become lay leaders in arthritis self-management programs. Volunteers enjoyed helping others with problems like their own, believed that they were involved in a worthwhile activity that gave life purpose and meaning, and took pride in their new status as lay leaders. Many of these first-time volunteers took a "leap of faith" to become involved. Afterward, they found themselves experiencing less pain and a greater willingness "to get on with life." Good health, then, is not a requirement for volunteering. The reverse, however, may be true.

❧ CONCLUSION

As one grows older and retires from work, things change. Friends and family may depart through death, sickness, or relocation. Influence over others and sometimes over one's own life may begin to lessen. Much of this is out of a person's control. Other people cannot always be controlled—nor can circumstances. What can be controlled, however, is what you do with the time that has been allotted to you—what activities you choose to become involved in. Deciding to give time, talents, and kindness to others by volunteering is an action fully under a person's control. Realizing that everyone right now has the power to change his or her own life and the lives of others toward well-being and health is empowering. What matters is not how big your gifts and abilities are, but rather that you use them to make life better for others. It's all about being faithful with whatever gifts you have, large or small—because the power comes from the purpose behind the actions, not from the results. In fact, you may never see the results of your volunteer activities—though they may endlessly reverberate through time and history.

CHAPTER 6

Cultivate Generosity

"Earn all you can, save all you can,
and then give all you can." —Charles H. Spurgeon

I N 1993, the median yearly household income in the United States was $36,746, by far the highest of any people in the world. By the year 2000, median household income had increased by 15 percent in real dollars to $42,148.[1] Truly, Americans are earning more than ever. Despite this abundance, however, they are saving less and giving less. As noted in chapter 2, according to a December 2001 CNN/Money report, Americans now save less than 1 percent of their incomes compared to 9 percent in 1994, and credit card debts are higher than ever before.[2] People are also giving less time and money to help those in need. Volunteering time to help others and cultivating an attitude of generosity are closely related. Generosity is admired in others, but it is a hard trait to develop. In this chapter, I will discuss why generosity is so important for living a full life. Much has been said about this topic.

Conrad N. Hilton (the founder of Hilton Hotels) made sure that his intentions to help others would be carried out long after his death by establishing the Hilton Foundation. This foundation has now awarded more than $330 million for charitable projects around the world. As part of his last will and testament, Hilton wrote the following:

There is a natural law, a Divine law, that obliges you and me to relieve the suffering, the distressed and the destitute. Charity is a supreme virtue, and the great channel through which the mercy of God is passed on to mankind. It is the virtue that unites men and inspires their noblest efforts. "Love one another, for that is the whole law"; so our fellow men deserve to be loved and encouraged—never to be abandoned to wander alone in poverty and darkness. The practice of charity will bind us—will bind all men in one great brotherhood.[3]

American aphorist Mason Cooley said, "Generosity knows how to count, but refrains." British biologist and educator Thomas Huxley said, "Thoughtfulness for others, generosity, modesty, and self-respect are the qualities which make a real gentleman, or lady, as distinguished from the veneered article which commonly goes by that name." The New Testament says, "You will be made rich in every way so that you can be generous on every occasion" (2 Corinthians 9:11). The Jewish Bible says, "The beneficent soul shall be made rich, and he that satisfieth abundantly shall be satisfied also himself" (Proverbs 11:25).

The Buddha emphasized that the origin of suffering in life is our own selfish desires, cravings for pleasure, and attempts to avoid pain. Consider some of the most prominent and well-known of his sayings: "Let us live most happily, possessing nothing; let us feed on joy, like the radiant gods" (Dhammapada 15.4). "The avaricious do not go to heaven, the foolish do not extol charity. The wise one, however, rejoicing in charity, becomes thereby happy in the beyond" (Dhammapada 13.11). "Giving is the noble expression of the benevolence of the mighty. Even dust, given in childish innocence, is a good gift. No gift that is given in good faith to a worthy recipient can be called small; its effect is so great" (Jatakamala 3.23). "Let the wise man do righteousness: a treasure that others cannot share, which no thief can steal: a treasure which does not pass away" (Khuddakapatha 8.9).[4]

In his classic work *Democracy in America*, a two-volume study of the American people and their political institutions, French politician and writer Alexis de Tocqueville wrote: "I have seen the freest and best-educated of men in circumstances the happiest to be found in the world. It seemed to me that a cloud habitually hung on their brow and they seemed serious and almost sad in their pleasures. They never stopped thinking of the good things they have not got. They clutch everything and hold nothing fast."

Do Americans hold onto their possessions too tightly, seeking more and more yet never having enough? "We are stripped bare by the curse of plenty," said Winston Churchill. Given the tremendous wealth that this nation and its inhabitants possess relative to other countries and people, are Americans really all that generous? Consider that the gross domestic product (GDP) of the United States (value of all final goods and services produced within a nation in a given year) with a population of 278 million was $10 trillion with a per capita GDP of $36,200 in the year 2000. Compare these numbers with similar figures for countries around the world, including Afghanistan with a per capita GDP of $800 (Table 6.1). If a person has food in the refrigerator, a roof overhead, and a place to sleep, he or she is richer than 75 percent of the world's population.[5] If a person has money in the bank and in his wallet, he is among 8 percent of the wealthiest people in the world. Many Americans may underestimate how much they really have. Eleanor Roosevelt said, "We cannot exist as a little island of well-being in a world where two-thirds of the people go to bed hungry every night." No, we cannot.

Where in the world does terrorism breed and flourish? It's in places like Afghanistan, Yemen, North Korea, and Iraq, some of the poorest countries with the lowest standards of living. Is it surprising that these people hate Americans who have so much and give so little in proportion to what they have? This nation has resources to dramatically reduce poverty and increase the standard of living of people around the world. As long as the United States refuses to do so, the threat of terrorism will never go away, since it will constantly resurface out of the ashes of poverty.

Table 6.1. Comparison of Gross Domestic Product to Economic Aid Given

Country	Population	National GDP	GDP Per Capita	Economic Aid[6]
United States	278,000,000	$10,000,000,000,000	$36,200	6,900,000,000 (.07%)
Japan	127,000,000	3,150,000,000,000	24,900	9,100,000,000 (.29%)
Canada	32,000,000	775,000,000,000	24,800	1,300,000,000 (.17%)
France	60,000,000	1,448,000,000,000	24,400	6,300,000,000 (.44%)
Germany	83,000,000	1,936,000,000,000	23,400	5,600,000,000 (.29%)
Australia	19,000,000	446,000,000,000	23,200	472,000,000 (.11%)
United Kingdom	60,000,000	1,360,000,000,000	22,800	3,400,000,000 (.25%)
Mexico	102,000,000	915,000,000,000	9,100	Receives assistance
Russia	145,000,000	1,120,000,000,000	7,700	Receives assistance
Brazil	174,000,000	1,130,000,000,000	6,500	NA (not available)
Iran	66,128,000	413,000,000,000	6,300	Receives assistance
Romania	22,000,000	133,000,000,000	5,900	NA (not available)
Philippines	83,000,000	310,000,000,000	3,800	Receives assistance
China	1,273,000,000	4,500,000,000,000	3,600	NA (not available)
Iraq	23,000,000	57,000,000,000	2,500	Receives assistance
India	1,030,000,000	2,200,000,000,000	2,200	Receives assistance
Pakistan	145,000,000	282,000,000,000	2,000	Receives assistance
Bangladesh	131,000,000	203,000,000,000	1,570	Receives assistance
Kenya	31,000,000	46,000,000,000	1,500	Receives assistance
Mozambique	19,000,000	19,000,000,000	1,000	Receives assistance
Sudan	36,000,000	36,000,000,000	1,000	Receives assistance
North Korea	22,000,550	22,600,000,000	1,000	Receives assistance
Nigeria	127,000,000	117,000,000,000	950	Receives assistance
Yemen	18,000,000	14,400,000,000	820	Receives assistance
Afghanistan	27,000,000	21,000,000,000	800	Receives assistance

(Source: World Factbook 2000)[7]

❧ DEFINITION

Roget's Thesaurus defines generosity as "The quality or state of being generous: big-heartedness, bounteousness, freehandedness, generousness, great-heartedness, large-heartedness, lavishness, liberality, magnanimity, magnanimousness, munificence, openhandedness, unselfishness, unsparingness." The *American Heritage Dictionary* defines it as "1. Liberality in giving or willingness to give: a scholarship funded by the generosity of anonymous donors. 2. Nobility of thought or behavior; magnanimity. 3. Amplitude; abundance. 4. A generous act." Both definitions convey a sense of freedom, greatness, and unselfish concern.

❧ WHO IS THE MOST GENEROUS?

Based on the limited criteria of how much money is given to charity and how much time is volunteered for charitable activities, who are the most generous in the United States?

According to a 1997–98 survey conducted by the Independent Sector,[8] a Washington, D.C.-based group that monitors charitable giving in the United States, the annual total contributions from private sources to nonprofits and religious organizations was $132 billion. The percentage of American households that gave was 70 percent, but 20 percent of households gave 70 percent of all contributions. The annual average household contribution was $754 (approximately 2.1 percent of annual income among those who gave). Among households that contributed, the average contribution was $1,075. The average contribution by households where at least one person was involved in volunteer work was $1,339, compared to $524 by non-volunteering households.

Interestingly, the poor give proportionally more than the rich. Those with incomes under $10,000 give 4.3 percent of income, double the national average.[9] College graduates give an average of 1.7 percent of their incomes.[10] Older adults give proportionally more than young adults (3.4 percent of income for those fifty-five to seventy-four years old versus 1.6 percent for those twenty-five to thirty-four).[11]

🌿 RELIGION AND GENEROSITY

The Christian Bible says, "Love is the fulfillment of the law" (Romans 13:8–10). Indeed, generosity is a form of love expressed toward others, and love is the ultimate commandment of the Christian Scriptures—it fulfills all the requirements, all of the rules. The Jewish Bible says, "Thou shalt not take vengeance, nor bear any grudge against the children of thy people, but thou shalt love thy neighbour as thyself: I am HaShem … " (Leviticus 19:18), and "The stranger that sojourneth with you shall be unto you as the home-born among you, and thou shalt love him as thyself; for ye were strangers in the land of Egypt: I am HaShem your G-d" (Leviticus 19:34). Christianity and Judaism are not alone in emphasizing the importance of love, which is a common and central theme of all major world religions. The big question, then, is the following: Are religious people more generous? The answer is an unqualified yes.

People who are more religious tend to be more generous with their finances. Of all predictors of giving, attendance at religious services is the best.[12] Regular attendees account for 80 percent of all giving. Weekly attendees gave 2.8 percent of their incomes, whereas those attending less than weekly gave 1.6 percent and non-attendees gave 1.1 percent. Among weekly church attendees, the average contribution in 1998 was $1,336 (compared to the average U.S. contribution of $754). Nevertheless, this amount actually declined slightly from a value of $1,386 in 1989. Likewise, the figure of 2.8 percent for weekly attendees in 1998 is down from 3.8 percent in 1989. When one considers that the 1998 figure applies to households during a time when the U.S. economy was booming, the drop in contributions since 1989 is significant.

As noted in the last chapter, religious persons also tend to be more generous with their time. Nearly one-half of those who attend religious services do volunteer work, compared to one-third of those who do not attend services. Unfortunately, most of this volunteering is confined to meeting needs in the religious community. Only 7–15 percent of volunteering done within religious organizations is directed toward meeting needs outside the religious community.[13]

❧ WAYS OF BEING GENEROUS

To what kinds of charitable causes do people give? In 1998, 60.1 percent of household contributions were made to the 354,000 religious organizations in the United States, 9.0 percent to human services, 6.5 percent to health, 6.4 percent to education, 4.9 percent to youth development, 3.3 percent to the arts, 3.2 percent to the environment, and 6.4 percent to other causes. People can be generous in ways other than donating money and possessions to help others, although financial and material giving is very important. Donating time, talents, and ideas by volunteering for good causes is another important way to be generous. What are some other ways?

Even those without a lot of money or free time can be generous. People can be generous with friendliness, consciously making an effort to smile and greet others warmly. President of the Association for Healthcare Philanthropy William C. McGinly said, "Giving a smile is a great gift. Smiles bring out the best in people. Smiles make people come alive, but you have to give yours away first." Don't just look for others who want to be friends—but rather take the initiative to be a friend to someone else. As author Anne S. Eaton said, "The investment of friendship pays higher dividends than any other investment you can make."

Be generous in thankfulness and praise and encouragement of others, whether they appear to deserve it or not. The great German poet Goethe said, "Treat someone as they really are, and they will become less than they are. Treat a person as they can be, and they will become that." Don't worry about genuinely thanking or praising people too much—it won't spoil them. Emily Post once said, "Praise, to be believed, must come often and with sincerity." Every person needs and craves such appreciation.

Be generous with kindness and compassion toward others. Kindness involves having a warm-hearted nature toward others, showing sympathy and understanding, being humane and considerate, demonstrating tolerance and patience with others. Compassion is being deeply aware of the suffering of another, desiring to relieve that suffering, and taking action based on that desire. As an old saying goes, "Sympathy sees, and says, 'I'm sorry.' Compassion sees, and whispers, 'I'll help.'" Compassion involves a willingness to suffer with another person, a willingness to carry the other person's burden—and do it with love, not feeling put upon for having to do it or feeling resentful for the inconvenience. Emerson once wrote, "[T]o know even one life has breathed easier because you have lived. That is to have succeeded."

People can be generous by listening. Allow another person to talk freely about what's bothering them without offering advice or giving an opinion. Listen intently and with focus—try to understand what the person is saying, try to get into their shoes for a while, experience what they are experiencing. Listening is powerful. Unfortunately, most people want themselves to be heard by others, want to express their own opinions, want to offer advice and fix problems that others have. To avoid this, many have to pay others to listen to them. Listening is the basis for all psychotherapy. Listening is how mental health professionals have healed psychological wounds for centuries. Showing restraint and offering another a chance to be heard and understood is a wonderful act of generosity. Writer Corrine U. Wells said, "The gifts of things are never as precious as gifts of thought."

People can be generous with common courtesies—holding the door when going in and out of restaurants or stores, being polite while driving on the freeway and when answering the telephone, and so on. Each of these actions shows generosity, kindness, and respect for others. Being generous in this way makes others feel good. Since it is so uncommon in today's society, people notice when others are generous with their courtesy and are attracted to them.

People can be generous with their prayers for others, and should let others know that they are praying for them. People can be generous giving spiritual support to others. Studies have shown that those who provide religious or spiritual help to others cope better with stress, experience less depression, and report a higher quality of life.[14] Being generous with prayer has measurable benefits for both the giver and the receiver.

People can be generous with their generosity. When giving to others, give with a friendly and enthusiastic manner—thereby communicating nonverbally that nothing is owed in return. Generosity should always be expressed in a loving manner. If it is done resentfully or grudgingly, much of the natural reward that comes from giving will be lost. Consider what the Christian Bible says about this: "If I speak in the tongues of men and of angels, but have not love, I am only a resounding gong or a clanging cymbal. If I have the gift of prophecy and can fathom all mysteries and all knowledge, and if I have a faith that can move mountains, but have not love, I am nothing. If I give all I possess to the poor and surrender my body to the flames, but have not love, I gain nothing" (1 Corinthians 13:1–3). No matter what a person does for others, no matter how much money someone gives or how much time someone volunteers, if it is not done with kindness and love, then nothing is gained by the giver—nothing.

❧ GENEROUS WITH WHOM?

English writer Thomas Browne said, "But how shall we expect charity towards others, when we are uncharitable to ourselves? Charity should begin at home." A prerequisite for being generous to others is that the needs of the family—physical, material, emotional, and social—are taken care of. Giving money to charity, helping others, or involvement in volunteer activities never justifies neglecting family members who require nurturance. This does not mean fulfilling all one's relatives' wishes, but rather being sure that their needs are met. After this has been accomplished, the next circle of generosity extends to friends and acquaintances. This includes neighbors in the local community, fellow church members, and those one may meet as part of business, work, or hobbies. Again, generosity extends beyond finances and time to include the other actions and attitudes described above—friendliness, kindness, compassion, listening, courtesy, praying with and for others.

The third ring of generosity extends to strangers and to those we've never met before. This might include the homeless at a local shelter or soup kitchen, the poor in the community, needy persons in other areas of the country or in disaster areas, and the poor in other countries such as India, Afghanistan, or poverty-stricken areas in Africa. Activities might include visiting shut-ins, needy persons in nursing homes, orphanages, or those with chronic illness, either at home or in the hospital.

The fourth ring of generosity extends to one's enemies. The Christian Scriptures encourage the love of enemies and doing good to those who persecute us. Seek to identify the needs of your enemies and reach out to them. They may not accept offers of help, but offering in a kind and generous way will nevertheless be appreciated—and if not appreciated, then it is still the right thing to do. If one is certain that an enemy will not accept help, then it may be better to help him indirectly so that he is not even aware of who is doing it. Such acts of kindness and generosity have a way of coming back around.

The fifth ring of generosity extends to God. "Gratitude to God makes even a temporal blessing a taste of heaven," said author William Romain. A person can be generous while spending time communicating with God in prayer, while receiving instruction from God when reading the Scriptures, and while worshiping God both alone and with others. This relationship becomes more important as one gets older, and will facilitate the transition from this life to the next.

❧ WHEN TO BE GENEROUS

Are there better times to be generous than others? Is there a special time and place or occasion? Here are some ideas about when to be generous.

First, be generous when others are being generous. These are times when you feel like being generous back. In that case, there is no need to restrain yourself—be richly generous back with appreciation. Second, be generous when people need help. Others' needs are not always convenient. They will occur at the most unexpected times and places. Try to be ready at all times— alert to the needs of others whenever they arise.

Third, be generous when people are unkind or hurtful. Physician-author Thomas Fuller said, "The noblest revenge is to forgive." Be generous with forgiveness, generous with your willingness to receive correction and admit error, generous with patience toward others and with a desire to understand. L. G. Harvey said, "When there is true understanding, forgiveness is not necessary." In other words, lack of forgiveness usually only displays one's ignorance of all the facts and circumstances. Complete knowledge of all the circumstances usually results in understanding, making forgiving a lot easier. Generosity when others are hurtful, however, does not come naturally, and may require a mobilization of the *will* to bring it about. Vince Lombardi said, "The difference between a successful person and others is not a lack of strength, not a lack of knowledge, but rather a lack of will." Generosity toward those who are hurtful is a way to exercise and strengthen the will.

Fourth, be generous when health and physical strength are vigorous, for then one is able to do many practical things for others, especially for those who are sick and less able. Take advantage of the blessing of physical health and use it to serve others.

Fifth, be generous when sick or disabled. When you are not feeling well, it will be more difficult to be generous and ways of being generous will be more limited. Nevertheless, even the sick and disabled can give to others—and they need more than ever to do so.

Sixth, be generous with acceptance when others are trying to help. Given the independent and self-sufficient spirit so widespread among Americans, many don't like receiving help from others. It makes some people feel dependent and indebted, which is a horrible feeling. However, humans need to be able to give and help others; sometimes, allowing people to help is actually a gift that can be given in return. As the old saying goes, "Love receives what love gives," and as the poet Leigh Hunt said, "To receive a present in a right spirit, even when you have none to give in return, is to give one in return." Thus, be generous with your acceptance of help—even when help is not really needed. And when it becomes possible to return the favor, return it generously; if it cannot be returned, then thank God and ask for special blessings on your helper—surely God has the ability and power to return such favors.

Finally, develop an attitude of generosity in every action—go beyond what others expect in terms of warmth, kindness, love, time, and practical acts of help. It is always the right time to be generous.

❧ GENEROUS, BUT NOT STUPID

There are also limits to generosity that need to be recognized and understood, particularly with regard to time, money, and physical and emotional stamina. You cannot volunteer for every cause, donate to every charity, or offer housing to all the homeless people you meet on the street. Attempts to do so will quickly result in burnout and lead to exhaustion. Always be sensitive to your own needs and limits, because they cannot be ignored indefinitely. The Christian Scriptures emphasize a balance of love of neighbor and love of self. The command is to love your neighbor as you love yourself—not less than yourself or more than yourself, but *as* yourself. For that reason, it is important to be generous toward yourself as well—not self-centered or self-indulgent, but generous in terms of forgiveness, understanding, and being willing to experience joy and simple pleasures as opportunities arise. God constantly wants to bless those who love and serve others, and those who serve should be willing to accept and enjoy blessings as they occur. As Jabez cried out in 1 Chronicles 4:10, "Oh that you would bless me, and enlarge my territory!"

❧ NEUROTIC REASONS
FOR GIVING AND RECEIVING

It is important to identify neurotic or self-serving reasons for helping others, volunteering, or donating money. Some people do these things for others because they are unable to do otherwise. In other words, they may feel so guilty or have such a psychological need to please others that they *cannot choose not to be generous*. In order to receive the benefits of generosity, one has to be free not to be generous. If some poor soul is forced into "generosity" by neurotic psychological needs, then the usual emotional rewards will not follow. These neurotic needs are often deep-seated and have their origins in childhood. Such early wounds or deprivations make a person unable to be selfish or focus on their own needs. In fact, such persons may feel anxious unless they are making others happy. As an extreme example, people in abusive relationships will go to great lengths in order to please or pacify the other person in the relationship, even if their partner is physically or emotionally hurtful and refuses to respect them or consider their needs. Helping for neurotic reasons is not associated with the joy and satisfaction that result from helping freely. Instead, the person who serves for neurotic reasons will feel stressed out and overwhelmed by doing things for others—and will soon come to resent it.

It is also important to determine when people are taking advantage of the generosity of others. These people are called "users." Friends, relatives, or strangers may seek to manipulate our good intentions, asking us to do things for them that they can and should do for themselves. They "use" people to serve their selfish wishes, not to fulfill needs that cannot be met in any other way. Such persons will be demanding, full of expectations, and often ungrateful—always taking and never giving back. They feel entitled—they feel that others "owe" them. These users may take advantage of a person's desire to help them and quickly drain good will and energy. Don't let them.

Recognize also when people need to do things for themselves in order to learn from a difficult situation or adapt to it. For example, a person may make a foolish business decision, lose money at the racetrack, or go to jail for committing a crime. To bail him out of such situations prevents him from learning from the natural consequences of his actions. Similarly, if you want to help a friend with arthritis, you may decide to provide for her needs so that she can stay sitting in her chair and won't have to get up and walk about to serve herself. However, by sitting in a chair and relying on others for everything, her muscles will become weaker and her joints more stiff and painful. Instead, it would be more helpful to encourage her to get up and do as much as she can for herself. Excessive helping can also make her dependent on the helper, so that she cannot function when the helper is not there. It is much better to do things that will help a person become more independent and functional and less dependent on others. As the old saying goes, "Give a man a fish and tomorrow he will go hungry; teach a man to fish, and tomorrow he will feed himself and his family."

Another point bears remembering as well. When being generous, always be generous with your own time and possessions—not with the resources of others. For example, while working on a job for someone else, don't take time to help people who are not connected with the job. This involves using an employer's time and resources to do good works, which the employer has not had a choice about. Another example is spending lots of time in volunteer work and neglecting duties around the house or ignoring your spouse. That time is not your own to give away. While others may be able to volunteer for a task, you have unique responsibilities to your family that others cannot fulfill. The same is true for donating money to worthy causes. If the money given to charitable causes does not entirely belong to the giver, it does not involve an act of giving but rather an act of stealing. For example, a husband may be donating money to charity that his family must have to live on, causing his wife and children's needs to go unmet. The money is not entirely his to give away. Be sure that whatever you give is entirely your own to give away.

❧ OTHER ASPECTS OF BEING GENEROUS

When being generous, it is also important not to expose yourself to unnecessary danger. For example, a young or middle-aged woman may wish to be generous by stopping to pick up a male hitchhiker or stranded motorist. In that situation, being generous may get the woman robbed, kidnapped, or even killed. Similarly, a person without a companion or adequate protection may decide to visit a poor family in a dangerous part of town Always be sensible and careful when volunteering help.

Finally, generosity should be done with sensitivity. Be alert to what others perceive their needs to be. Follow their guidance on how to help them. Don't impose generosity on others because of your need to do so. Rather, be focused on their needs and preferences. Find out from them what they want and what they need, and don't assume. Be sensitive, ask questions, and respond to the needs of others as *they* perceive them.

❧ HOW TO BE MORE GENEROUS

I have struggled with generosity my entire life. I was raised in a family that did not give much money or time to helping others. My family's focus was on accumulating wealth and possessions and taking care of "Number One." I had no early role models and so I have battled with this issue for years. How does a person learn to become more generous when his or her natural bent is otherwise? I don't have all the answers, but the following activities may help.

First, read about how important generosity is. Read the teachings of prophets and saints whose writings have lasted for thousands of years. These wise men and women must have captured a bit of truth, since their teachings have withstood the test of time and met the needs of generation after generation. What is said about generosity in the Jewish Scriptures, the New Testament, the Quran, the Bhagavad-Gita, and the writings of the Buddha and Confucius (see chapter 10)? These writings span a period of over four thousand years—and yet they send the same message. How can they all be wrong, mistaken about the key to a victorious, meaningful, and joyous life?

Second, spend time with people who are generous. They are

not easy to find, and when you find one, there will be plenty of competition to befriend him or her. Generous people naturally attract others because of their generosity, and it is not always financial generosity. Some people simply have generous spirits that make others feel good in their presence.

The single person who has impressed me the most with his generosity is Sir John Templeton. I have worked around this man for the past seven years, and have seen how he treats people—especially ordinary people. He is generous and genuine in his interest in each person he meets. He makes considerable effort to learn about what in life excites people—what they spend their time on, what their dreams are. He is a generous tipper, not to impress but to share with those less fortunate out of his abundance. He gives generously to needy causes. He is also generous with his ideas, his vision, and his desire to do good.

Even more important, he is kind and considerate, a real gentleman who gives respect to others. He is generous in his praise and encouragement and therefore brings out the best in people. Goethe said, "Correction does much, but encouragement does more. Encouragement after censure is as the sun after a shower." That is Sir John. He is a powerhouse of purpose, optimism, and positive thinking, believing that anything is possible. His entire life has been a testament to the wise saying of investment counselor Elaine Rideout: "Ignore people who say it can't be done." How many extremely wealthy persons in this world have devoted their entire fortunes to promoting forgiveness, gratitude, thankfulness, character building, increased spirituality, and knowledge about God? And how many of them are eighty-nine years old and still doing it?

Third, plan to be generous. During your pre-retirement years, begin to finance retirement so that both time and financial resources will be available to give to others. Confucius said, "When prosperity comes, do not use all of it." If a person enters into retirement strapped financially, then simply living from day to day may take up all his or her time and there will be little money available to give to others. Savings for retirement can almost all be tax deferred and will reduce taxable income. Planning should really start in early adulthood, although few have the foresight at that time. Middle age, when most people are at the peak of their careers and earning potential, is the next best time to start investing for retirement.

Planning for retirement, however, will not by itself make a person more generous—it will only make him or her more capable of being generous. Some people never make it to the point that they actually start giving. As nineteenth-century minister and slavery foe William Ellery Channing once said, "We must not waste life in devising means. It is better to plan less and do more." Therefore, fourth, begin to practice being generous right now. Many people delay this, saying that one day—when they are more economically secure—they will be more generous with their time and money. That will never happen.

A person will never be economically secure enough until he or she actually begins to practice generosity. Somehow, being generous reduces one's anxiety about financial security. Being generous makes people feel richer, wealthier, and less in need of more wealth. It also makes them less dependent on their wealth for security. This feeling of security cannot be obtained by accumulating more and more wealth. That is why a person needs to start being generous now, or will likely never be. Experiencing the benefits of generosity will help establish a habit of it. This does not mean that those who are already retired can't start being generous, but that the time to start is now, retired or not.

Finally, commit to being generous even if there are no immediate benefits. Most benefits from generosity come later and often when you are least expecting them. The long-term benefits to character, spiritual maturity, and emotional security are the big payoffs, and they usually occur long after the good deeds are done. However, they keep paying off because generosity changes a person. The generous person likes himself more and others like him a lot better as well. Benefits will also come from completely unexpected sources. Careful study can often connect these payoffs with previous acts of kindness and generosity. Remember again that generosity does not involve only money or volunteering, but also the way that one treats others. Friendliness, compassion, understanding, patience, and forgiveness all bring greater joy to life, and they are the fruits of a generous attitude and spirit.

❧ CONCLUSION

Americans have so much more than most people in the world, yet they often feel that they do not have enough. That's because a person's "need" is not filled by acquiring more things, more toys, more money, but rather by giving to and investing in the lives of others. Giving is what makes us feel whole. Author Arnold Glasow sums it up well: "Doing things just for our own good seldom does us any." Making generosity a goal and reality is a sure way to experience power in retirement. Generosity requires a certain degree of maturity that is usually not achieved until enough experience has accumulated to recognize that a self-absorbed life is not very fulfilling.

Often it is not until later in life that a person cries out in existential despair: "Is there any more to life than this?" The answer is yes—there is more, but it's only accessible by cultivating a spirit of generosity. It takes a spirit of generosity to get to the next level. Perhaps it is at the next level that everyone is intended be—and anyone who remains selfish and self-absorbed, especially during the final years of life, soon begins to experience a lack. That "lack" is a call to the next level. I think it's a spiritual call, a nudge from a loving Creator who wants his creatures to experience the best and the most that life can give.

CHAPTER 7

Develop Spiritually

"Our Father in heaven, hallowed be your name,
Your kingdom come, your will be done on earth as it is in heaven."
—*Matthew 6:9–10*

O NE ALTERNATIVE to seeking pleasure and leisure in retirement is deciding to spend time developing the spiritual side of life. Why is this important? To put it plainly, spirituality is one of the most readily available sources of purpose during the second half of life. Taking time to volunteer or being financially generous is very difficult to do—regardless of the intrinsic rewards promised. Something else is required to change and transform people so that they are willing and able to stop focusing on themselves and to start focusing on the needs of others. In my opinion, nothing comes even close to spirituality in enabling that transformation. Spirituality is motivating, energizing, and inspiring, so developing spiritually can make a real difference during retirement. Frankly, I don't see how real purpose is possible without it. Even that archenemy of religion Sigmund Freud had to admit: "[O]nly religion can answer the question of the purpose of life. One can hardly be wrong in concluding that the idea of life having a purpose stands and falls with the religious system."[1]

All major world religions and other strong value-based belief systems provide purpose and meaning that can help their followers maintain mental and physical health after retirement. I include examples of resources toward the end of this chapter that explore spirituality in Christian, Jewish, Islamic, and Eastern traditions. As an in depth example here, however, I will discuss the influence that Christian spirituality has on the development of purpose and meaning.

My focus on Christianity does not mean that other religious traditions (or nonreligious philosophies) cannot provide powerful motivation and direction that give meaning to the changes that occur with aging, but only that the Judeo-Christian tradition is the one with which I am most familiar and can therefore address from firsthand experience. This firsthand experience is especially necessary since I have no formal theological training. Thus, the views I present here on spirituality are as a physician and as a mental health specialist, not as a learned theologian. I am relying primarily on what I've learned caring for people with emotional problems and conducting research on mental health and aging, my relatively superficial knowledge of Judeo-Christian Scriptures, and personal experience gained by struggling through a not-always-easy life. I come from a conservative Christian background and that further colors this discussion (and no doubt has already colored what I have written thus far). A bit more about my personal background will help the reader understand my perspective even further.

When I turned fifty, I knew that my Christian faith would play a major role in my search for purpose and meaning during my pre-retirement and retirement years. The reason why I was so certain about this was the role that both Catholic and Protestant Christianity had played in shaping my life and career up to that point. Until I reached the age of thirty-three, my life had little aim or purpose; it was pretty much a wandering journey of failures and disappointments. Like many of my friends, I was seeking worldly things that seemed to evaporate as I desperately reached out to grasp them. Oh, sure, I had graduated from medical school and was on my way to a successful career. But there was something missing in my life, a void that I could not fill no matter what I did. I thought that finding a mate and companion would bring my life together and make me happy. However, I was repeatedly let down.

I began to wonder why I was here. There had to be more to life than work, accumulating things, getting married, raising kids, socializing with friends, growing old, becoming sick, and then dying. Was there anything more to this brief life? I was a seeker.

It was not until my own emotional pain forced me to turn to the Christian Scriptures for answers that I finally found some. Within a few months of reading the Bible, I was transformed. I had a new vision for my life, a greater purpose for my existence, and the energy and motivation to realize that vision. It was then that I felt "called" into the area of gerontology and aging. I was also greatly influenced by Robert Butler's book, *Why Survive?* The book talked about the plight of the elderly in America. With that call to the mission field of America's elderly came a new direction. Boredom and loneliness started to diminish as I began to develop spiritually and became more involved in gerontology. Slowly I began to experience more and more excitement and meaning in my work and in my relationships.

For seventeen years now I have tried to make spiritual development a priority, sometimes with more and sometimes with less success. When I keep a spiritual focus, it directs my steps, determines my goals, enables me to become more loving and caring, more kind and compassionate, more forgiving and understanding. When I lose that focus, as I so often do, the opposite occurs. It is then that I begin to re-experience the anxiety, worry, restlessness, and obsessive self-preoccupation of my youth. Before long, the emotional turmoil and the negative trials and circumstances of life soon force my attention back to spiritual matters. For me, then, spirituality is not a casual option, but a necessity for my survival. It's my own answer to the question "Why survive?"

❧ PURPOSE IN THE SCRIPTURES

Looking back, I now realize my new sense of purpose and direction came about because of my studying the Scriptures. Indeed, the Judeo-Christian Scriptures have a lot to say about purpose. From the very start, human beings were created with a purpose in mind. "Then God said, 'Let us make man in our image, in our likeness, and let them rule over the fish of the sea and the birds of the air, over the livestock, over all the earth'" (Genesis 1:26). That verse taught me that human beings have a purpose and that purpose is to rule over all the earth, which means to take care of everything on the earth, including other people— those who are hungry or without shelter, and those who are lonely or without hope. Humans were created to be responsible for others. Cain revolted against this idea. "Am I my brother's keeper?" he asked God (Genesis 4:9). God's answer to that question was yes.

The prophets in the Hebrew Testament each believed they had a purpose. That purpose was their calling. When they lost their purpose, no matter how much they had already accomplished, they often became depressed and useless. Consider the prophet Elijah who, after defeating the nine hundred prophets of Baal and Asherah, lost his sense of purpose and lay down to die. "He came to a broom tree, sat down under it and prayed that he might die. 'I have had enough, LORD,' he said. 'Take my life; I am no better than my ancestors'" (1 Kings 19:4). It was not until God himself appeared to Elijah and reminded him of his purpose that he straightened out. "'What are you doing here, Elijah?... Go back the way you came...'" (1 Kings 19:9, 15). Elijah then went back and anointed the new king of Israel. He had rediscovered his purpose—with God's help.

Jesus also came to earth with a purpose. Describing that purpose he said, "For the Son of Man came to seek and to save what was lost" (Luke 19:10). What was it that was lost and needed saving? It was humanity. They had lost their way, and Jesus came to help them find it again. He came to give people worthy goals to strive for in order to save them from themselves, from their obsessive preoccupation with their own needs, wants, and desires. Instead, Jesus said not to accumulate treasures here on earth but rather to accumulate them in heaven. "Do not store up for yourselves treasures on earth, where moth and rust destroy, and where thieves break in and steal. But store up for yourselves treasures in heaven, where moth and rust do not destroy, and where thieves do not break in and steal. For where your treasure is, there your heart will be also" (Matthew 6:19–21). Jesus taught his followers not to focus exclusively on themselves, but to place their attention on God and on loving others. "Love the Lord your God with all your heart and with all your soul and with all your strength and with all your mind; and love your neighbor as yourself" (Luke 10:27). Jesus said not to ignore those in need, but rather to help them and do so as if serving Jesus himself. "I tell you the truth, whatever you did for one of the least of these brothers of mine, you did for me" (Matthew 25:40).

Then consider the apostle Paul. This is how he describes his purpose: "Forgetting what is behind and straining toward what is ahead, I press on toward the goal to win the prize for which God has called me heavenward" (Philippians 3:13–14). Straining toward the goal to win the prize, with single-mindedness and focus, is like an athlete running with all of his strength and power to reach the finish line—that was Paul. Yes, there is much in Scripture about the importance of purpose.

🌿 SPIRITUAL DEVELOPMENT

Let me now describe my understanding of what spiritual development means from a Christian perspective, based on a rather simple knowledge of Judeo-Christian Scriptures. I don't think it means growing closer to nature, becoming more artistic, or acquiring more knowledge. I don't think it means growing more broadly and diffusely spiritual in ways that are hard to pin down, that focus only on feeling good, or that avoid all responsibility and accountability to others. Spiritual development, as I use the term here, involves three potential areas of growth.

First, spiritual development has to do with growing closer to God, and that closeness involves becoming more dependent on and trusting of God. The divine relationship is so important because that is where the power comes from that runs the motor that drives purpose. Second, spiritual development involves a growing love for one's neighbors that includes a commitment to their well-being and a willingness to suffer, if necessary, to help meet their needs (with "neighbor" being defined as almost anyone—family, friends, and strangers). The behavior that involves loving others is important because this is how a person actually carries out divine purpose. Third, spiritual development involves a deeper appreciation for and acceptance of oneself as God's child, created with a special purpose and irreplaceable in God's overall plan. This is important because it is impossible to love and serve others unless one has a comfortable sense of self and appreciation for one's identity as a loved child of God. In summary, spiritual development and its ultimate goal, spiritual maturity, mean achieving a balanced focus on God, on others, and on self, in that order. That threefold focus directs the will of the spiritually mature person.

❧ SPIRITUALITY AND PURPOSE

Spirituality can become a solid basis for purpose during retirement. As one advances in age, other sources of purpose tend to fade and lose power. Consider the well-known agnostics and atheists throughout history—Bertrand Russell, Arthur Schopenhauer, Friedrich Nietzsche, Ernest Hemingway, and others.[2] Many experienced a profound loss of purpose and identity as they began to battle with old age. Their highly rational, secular world-views gave little comfort and seemed to lose power as they aged. Spirituality can provide the older person with direction (where to go), power (the ability to go), and wisdom (how to go).

Direction. Spirituality gives life direction and focus. Spirituality helps to direct attention to needs in the world, needs that a person may have the gifts and talents to fulfill. Spirituality gently prompts and urges us to perform specific acts of kindness, service, and compassion toward others. When a person responds to such prompting, he or she is enabled to actually participate in the divine plan. Spirituality gives these acts of kindness and mercy special meaning and significance. Each is transformed into an act of service to the Creator. What greater task could human energies be directed toward? A life that is self-focused quickly begins to shrink as one experiences loss of health, loss of loved ones, and loss of status in society. However, as human goals come into closer alignment with the divine will, horizons broaden and the world begins to expand, not shrink, with increasing age. Boredom and uselessness are replaced by a sense of vision, a worthy vision that can serve as a target for the rest of life. The poet Betsey Kline said, "It takes courage to trust in God's leading, and make his will our own, but it is foolish to go the way alone."

Power. As a person develops spiritually, it allows him or her to increasingly tap into a source of divine power far greater than he or she would otherwise have access to because of limited human capacity. Divine power can drive our actions and propels us ahead—filling our lives with excitement, direction, and meaning. Spirituality fires up a person. What is the basis for that fire in Christianity? Samuel Brengle, long-time minister in the Salvation Army, wrote: "It is love. It is faith. It is hope. It is passion, purpose, determination—utter devotion. It is singleness of eye and a consecration unto death. It is God the Holy Ghost burning in and through a humble, holy, faithful person." Again, power comes from the relationship with the divine. When purpose is based on spiritual faith, it makes a person enthusiastic about what he does, and "Enthusiasm," according to Henry Chester, "is the greatest asset in the world. It beats money and power and influence." Interestingly, *enthusiasm* is derived from a Greek word that means to be inspired or possessed by God.

Wisdom. Wisdom helps to guide the energy from spirituality that propels a person forward in fulfilling his or her purpose. Spiritual involvement gives wisdom on how to spend time and resources in a way that most effectively accomplishes goals and realizes the vision set before him or her. The spiritual person is allowed to share in divine wisdom as he or she aligns his or her will with the divine will. The veil of ignorance is lifted as the spiritual person learns how the experiences of the past have prepared him or her to be used as a tool in the hands of the divine. Spiritual people become humble as they come into greater contact with divine wisdom, realizing the limits of their knowledge, abilities, and personal desires.

The Joy of Purpose-filled Serving

One of the greatest and deepest joys that humans of any age can experience is serving God by meeting the needs of others. The reason, I believe, is that God loves his children and hates to see them suffering and in pain. Because of this, when a person reaches out to help others, he can be absolutely certain that he is in God's will. What a great feeling it is to really know beyond a shadow of a doubt that one is doing God's will, even if it takes a lot of energy and work. When the motive is right (no expectation of reward, done only out of service to and love for God), there is no other feeling quite like it. Pleasure from leisure or recreation doesn't come close. Of course, as discussed earlier, if such service is based on a neurotic need to please others or is based on an unhealthy self-concept, meeting the needs of others becomes a burden and anything but fulfilling or joyful. Joy from service to others also receives a real boost if one has a meaningful relationship with God, because much of the reward comes out of that relationship.

Is this a naïve understanding of spirituality and the kind of purpose that it can give? Perhaps. It is certainly not very sophisticated or based on much philosophical or theological understanding, but rather on a simple attempt to synthesize what I have discovered in Scripture, experienced through life, and learned about in my studies of mental health and human behavior. The notion of deciding to love God, others, and self, and making this the basis for living, seems to be an idea that cuts across most denominations within Christianity and to some extent even transcends other belief systems. Other religions in the world—especially the other great monotheistic traditions—believe in a God and a Creator who has a will and plan for this earth, who can be known in a personal way, and who includes people in his divine will and plan. Assuming for the moment that the notions about spirituality and purpose described above are somehow rooted in reality, how can an individual know if he or she is developing spiritually? Are there any signs to watch out for?

❧ HOW CAN YOU TELL?

Fruits should accompany spiritual development. They are indicators of spiritual maturity and ought to be observable. Those fruits involve becoming more forgiving, more understanding, more patient, more kind, more compassionate, more giving, more generous—toward God, neighbor, and self. It's impossible to fake these fruits of the Spirit (Galatians 5:22), which provide objective evidence of progress.

Immediately after listing these traits, however, I realize how difficult they are to demonstrate. In particular, I realize that I've been failing more often than not in this regard. Nevertheless, I believe that such a struggle, with slow advances forward interrupted often by large steps backward, is typical. In fact, the struggle itself is evidence of spiritual development—of a desire to grow in this area. All the spiritual giants of the past struggled with their human natures and depended on help from outside themselves. Ignatius of Loyola, founder of the Jesuit religious order, prayed: "Teach us, good Lord, to serve thee as Thou deservest: to give and not to count the cost; to fight and not to heed the wounds; to toil and not to seek for rest; to labor and not to ask for any reward save that of knowing that we do Thy will." Even Jesus got angry and frustrated with others, disobeyed his parents a time or two, and cursed a fig tree when it disappointed him. Yes, all struggle and need lots of grace for this journey.

Each person will also start from a different place on the journey. Some people have so much baggage from the past involving circumstances of childhood, inherited temperament, and negative experiences in adulthood that they may seem spiritually immature to an outside observer—but in reality, they may have come a very long way. Others with many resources at their disposal and few barriers to overcome may seem spiritually mature and yet actually may not have come very far at all. So no one but the all-knowing Creator is truly aware of how much progress any one person has made in becoming spiritually mature and can therefore judge. Spiritual growth is all about progress and change and struggle, not about the particular place you are located on the path. Spiritual purpose is what gives direction and power for growth and change.

❧ CONSEQUENCES OF A SPIRITUAL LIFE

There have been attempts to study the consequences of a spiritual life. The crude methods of social science and medical research, of course, provide a very incomplete picture—only the tip of the iceberg, in my opinion—but enough at least to give us a glimpse of the possibilities. This has been my area of research for almost twenty years, so I'm now finally getting around to a subject that I'm an expert on.

Religious and spiritual beliefs are frequently used to help cope with stress. As the old saying goes, "Faith is what helps us to face the music even when we don't like the tune." Nearly seventy-five studies to date have examined the use of religion by those facing disabling medical illness, chronic mental illness, the death of a loved one, natural disasters, and other stressful circumstances.[3] Perhaps the clearest example of this is the response of the American people to the September 11, 2001, terrorist attacks. In a study published in the *New England Journal of Medicine*, a telephone survey of a large random sample of Americans found that 90 percent turned to religion to cope. This response was given more frequently than any other coping behavior except talking with friends or relatives about the event.[4]

Not only is there evidence that many cope with stress using religious or spiritual beliefs, but research shows that those people who depend on religion to cope actually do better than those who don't depend on religion. Nearly five hundred studies report that persons who are more involved in religious and spiritual practices experience greater well-being, life satisfaction, peace, and hope, are more optimistic, more forgiving, more altruistic, less depressed and anxious, less likely to commit suicide, and generally live fuller and happier lives.[5] Thus, it does appear that when objectively studied, those who are more religious experience more of the "fruits" described above. Of course, not everyone who is deeply spiritual is completely happy or free of suffering. In fact, true spiritual growth often does not occur until suffering and adversity stretch a person beyond his or her own resources.[6]

In addition to being associated with greater well-being and

better coping, religious involvement is also linked with better physical health and longer survival. It appears that spiritual development leads to both a better life and a longer one as well. Systematic research is showing that religious beliefs and practices likely have physical consequences—lower blood pressure, less heart disease, stronger immune functioning, and quicker recovery from illness.[7] The explanation for at least part of this effect lies in the mind-body relationship. Because those who are more religious or spiritual have better mental health, greater well-being, and experience less stress, this could reduce the frequency of stress-related illnesses—and stress-related illnesses are among the most common causes of disease and death in the world today.[8]

Another reason for the effect could have to do with greater social support. Spiritually involved people have more friends, larger social networks, and report a higher quality of support than do those who are not religious. Social support helps to reduce stress even further and improves disease monitoring and treatment compliance.

Finally, religious people live healthier lives and make healthier decisions—they don't smoke as much, drink as much, or involve themselves in risky practices such as drinking and driving, driving without seatbelts fastened, or engaging in unsafe sexual practices.[9] Thus, spiritual beliefs and behaviors likely influence both physical health and longevity.

Spiritually involved people also approach death and dying with less fear and with more security and confidence. Because they are not paralyzed by such concerns in their later years, the devoutly religious are able to live with hope and optimism to the very end of their lives, believing that death is not the end but only the beginning of a new and better existence. This allows those who are growing older to live to the fullest, even when they become sick and disabled, because they know that what awaits them is not a permanent end to all experience, but a homecoming—when they will once again join their loved ones and friends who have gone before them.

Those who are spiritually active also look forward when they die to being with God, whom they have come to know during this life as a friend and supporter. Then they will experience God fully and completely, which will be the ultimate experience of joy and healing. Yes, a homecoming. How different this view is from the view of those who have no hope of eternal life, who believe death is the final end, who see the pain and suffering that precede death as having no purpose or meaning.

❧ FURTHER READING

The Christian pathway I've focused on in this chapter provides only one viewpoint within one particular religion on how spirituality can bring purpose and power during retirement. Many resources can further spiritual development and contribute to a sense of meaning and purpose in later life. These are written from a Christian, Jewish, Islamic, and Eastern perspective, depending on the reader's preference. Below is a sample of some of the best books now in print on spiritual development.

For Christian spirituality, the first one I recommend is *The Living Bible*.[10] Although it paraphrases the biblical text, this is the easiest version of the Bible to read, making it possible to get through the entire book in a relatively short time. Reading the entire Bible from cover to cover provides a tremendous perspective on the Judeo-Christian faith—the struggles faced by the Jewish people, their successes and failures, God's faithfulness over time, the life and death of Jesus, and the writings of the apostles. The problems encountered and overcome in the Bible are human problems that have changed little over time, since human nature remains largely the same. The solutions to problems of living and relating to one another have not changed much either.

Closer Than a Brother[11] is a small book originally written by a monk named Brother Lawrence (1611-1691). This modern version provides key insights on how to develop a closer relationship with God. It is easy to read and offers practical suggestions on how to live in God's presence throughout the day, even at work (Brother Lawrence worked in a hospital kitchen). *The Imitation of Christ* is another profoundly spiritual book that helps to form attitudes based on time-tested ways of viewing reality.[12] While it is a bit harsh in places because the writer is an ascetic monk, the volume is full of wisdom and truth.

I also like *The Joy in Loving*, which is a compilation of sayings by Mother Teresa of Calcutta.[13] *The Pilgrim's Progress* by John Bunyan is a powerful work that describes the faith journey of a Christian pilgrim though life after a transforming spiritual experience and the many trials and temptations that he faced.[14] For the spiritual seeker wishing to have an intellectual explanation of Christianity, there is nothing better than *Mere Christianity* and all of C. S. Lewis's works.[15]

Other books that nurture Christian spiritual development include *In His Steps*[16] (a book about a town that decides to radically follow the teachings of Jesus after a homeless man challenges a local congregation), *Hinds' Feet on High Places*[17] (an allegory about a young disabled girl who is led and directed through life by Jesus), and of course, *The Prayer of Jabez*[18] (based on a little-known Old Testament figure's prayer that has become an international best-seller). Finally, *Affliction* by Edith Schaeffer is a powerful and moving volume about how to transform the pain of physical suffering into an experience with meaning and possibility.[19]

For the Jewish spiritual seeker, there is *Finding a Spiritual Home*[20] by Sid Schwarz, which addresses how contemporary synagogues can meet the needs of Jews who are looking for community and a spiritual connection to Judaism. Schwarz, emeritus rabbi of Adat Shalom in Bethesda, Maryland, has spent the past twenty years in search of synagogues that respond to the needs of today's Jews, and this book describes his findings. *Endless Light* by David Aaron explores the fundamental and universally troubling questions that retired persons often struggle with.[21] Aaron, head of the Isralight Institute in Jerusalem, seeks answers to questions of purpose and meaning in life as revealed in the kabbalah, the mystical teachings used to interpret the Torah. Finally, there is *Back to the Sources: Reading the Classic Jewish Texts*,[22] which articulates basic Jewish teachings on many subjects.

For the Muslim spiritual seeker, *The Koran* continues to be one of the best present-day translations of the Holy Quran. Written by world-renowned Islamic scholar N. J. Dawood, this translation has had many revisions since its first appearance in the mid-1950s and is the only translation of the sacred text produced by a major U.S. publishing house.[23] *The Holy Quran* by Maulana Muhammad Ali, first published in 1917, provides the Arabic text and English translation in parallel columns, along with notes underneath that explain the meanings of important words and make connections with previous passages. The translation is said to be more faithful to the Arabic original than other translations in print.[24] Over 250 of the works of Islam's greatest poet are presented in *Gift: Poems by Hafiz the Great Sufi Master*.[25] These poems illustrate the wisdom, love, generosity, and humor of this great spiritual teacher.

For those who are not sure which spiritual direction they wish to take, *The Long Journey Home* and *The Call* by Os Guinness are thought-provoking, intellectually challenging, and very well written.[26] Karen Armstrong's *A History of God: The 4000-Year Quest for Judaism, Christianity and Islam*, a best-seller for almost a decade, explores the ways in which the idea and experience of God has developed in Jews, Christians, and Muslims.[27] Armstrong is perhaps the most articulate, elegant, and thoughtful of religious historians. *The Relaxation Response* and *Timeless Healing* by Harvard cardiologist Herbert Benson[28] discuss the powerful physiological effects of meditation on the body and describe spiritual experiences that people have had during deep meditative states. For Eastern spiritual seekers, there are the works of the Dalai Lama, such as *An Open Heart: Practicing Compassion in Everyday Life* and, perhaps his most famous work, *The Art of Happiness: A Handbook for Living.*[29] These books, written by a giant among spiritual teachers, are quick reading and inspirational.

🌿 CONCLUSION

The prophet Isaiah talks about those who are advancing in years and God's purpose for them. God says, speaking through Isaiah, "Even to your old age and gray hairs I am he, I am he who will sustain you. I have made you and will carry you; I will sustain you and I will rescue you" (Isaiah 46:4). Retirement is a time of change—sometimes massive change—involving health and independence, family relationships, friendships, and position in society. Spiritual development will help to buffer these changes, maintain physical and mental health, and energize and direct individuals to carry out activities that will give purpose, power, and significance.

Spirituality levels the playing field in terms of health and age. The sick or disabled are no longer at a disadvantage. Everyone who is conscious and capable of exerting his or her will—even if it occurs only through silent prayer—has the potential to play an important part in carrying out the divine plan. Most important is the desire to serve and the decision to offer up one's abilities (whatever they may be). As the human will joins together with the divine will, power begins to flows through the individual and a transformation takes place. That transformation can turn retirement into the most meaningful years of life.

CHAPTER 8

Reduce Stress

---

*"There is no fear in love. But perfect love
drives out fear."* — 1 John 4:18

I HAVE REFERRED OFTEN to the word stress in the preceding chapters—implying that it is not something good and that it sometimes increases with advancing age. Stress has become a buzzword in society today. Everyone seems to be stressed over something, whether they are retired or not, old or young. It has been said, "A day of worry is more exhausting than a week of work." Stress eats away at joy and power for living. What exactly is stress, and what are some sources of it? What are the effects of stress on the physical body that explain why it is so important to keep it under control? How does one reduce stress during retirement, and how does this relate to purpose in the retirement years?

❧ WHAT IS STRESS?

Stress can be either external or internal. External stress is any threat to the integrity of the physical body caused by the weather, intense exercise, starvation, or being in a dangerous environment like war or under attack by a wild animal. Internal stress results from the amazing and truly unique ability that humans have as conscious beings. They are able to anticipate with fear negative things that might happen to them in the future or remember with regret terrible things that happened to them in the past. I will focus here on internal stress.

What most people don't realize is that the consequences of internal stress created by negative emotions such as anxiety, fear, worry, or sense of time pressure are almost exactly the same as those caused by external threats to the physical body. Other negative emotions such as depression, anger, resentment, or lack of forgiveness also cause internal stress. Even boredom or a sense of uselessness can generate internal stress that has negative consequences for health and well-being. Thus, it doesn't much matter whether stress results from an external threat to the physical body or an internal threat to the psychological self—the negative biological effects on the body remain exactly the same. This is because the brain and nervous system cannot distinguish threats to the physical body from threats to the psychological self.

Our perception or interpretation of events largely determines how stressful they are. An event that is very stressful for one person may evoke enjoyment and excitement for another. For example, parachuting out of an airplane might be terrific fun for a skydiver, but is likely to evoke terror for someone not experienced in this activity. Stress is often determined by the amount of control and choice that a person has in a particular situation. Loss of control and limited choices increase the magnitude of stress experienced. Stress is particularly high when people are in difficult situations that they can do nothing about.

❧ EFFECTS OF STRESS ON THE BODY

The fight-or-flight response is a reaction that humans have in common with almost all living creatures, even lowly snails and mollusks. It apparently developed very early during the evolutionary process. The fight-or-flight response consists of a series of physiological changes that ensures an organism's physical survival in a hostile environment. Discovered by Walter Cannon in the 1930s, the fight-or-flight response is set into motion whenever the individual perceives danger.[1] Any life experience considered threatening to a person's physical body or psychological self will elicit the response. Thus, as noted earlier, it's not just physical danger that elicits the response, but also when a person experiences a psychological or social threat to self-image, self-identity, or self-esteem. What occurs is described below.

The instant that danger to the self is perceived, at least two areas of the brain are flooded with nerve signals—the locus ceruleus and the hypothalamus.[2] The nerve cells in the locus ceruleus then begin to send signals down long nerve tracks from the brain through the spinal cord down to clusters of nerve cells (called sympathetic ganglia) alongside the spinal column. These nerve cells, in turn, send signals down nerve fibers that encircle the blood vessels, the heart, the stomach, the intestines, and other vital internal organs. Within a second or less after the threat is perceived, blood flow is redirected from the skin, intestines, and other organs (where it is not needed to respond to the immediate threat) to the large muscles, heart, and brain (organs necessary for fighting or running). At the same time, signals are sent down nerve fibers that circle and penetrate the adrenal medulla, (glands that sit on top of the kidneys). The adrenal medulla respond to these signals by injecting large amounts of adrenaline into the bloodstream, which makes the heart beat more quickly and forcefully, increases blood pressure, and maximizes alertness—again, all with the intention of preparing the body physiologically to fight off or escape from whatever is threatening the person.

At the same time that the locus ceruleus is activating blood vessels, heart, and adrenal medulla, the hypothalamus and pituitary gland in the brain are releasing hormones such as corticotropin-releasing hormone and adrenocorticotropic hormone.

These hormones travel in the bloodstream to a special part of the adrenal glands called the adrenal cortex. Responding to these hormones in the blood, cells in the adrenal cortex release corticosteroids (or steroids) into the bloodstream. These steroids then go through the blood to the large muscles of the arms and legs, increasing their strength and maximizing their function. Athletes such as weightlifters sometimes inject themselves with steroids so that their muscles will be stronger and they will be more competitive. It's all based on the same principle.

Steroids also do another thing that is very energy efficient in the short term, thereby freeing up energy for the muscles, heart, and brain to take immediate action. The steroids help to shut down immune functioning. Why does this help? The immune system uses up lots of energy. This drains energy away from organs that need it to fight off or escape from whatever is threatening the individual. Imagine what happens when a person becomes sick with a cold. The person begins to feel tired and experiences a great need to rest and sleep because the immune system is working very hard to rid the body of the cold virus, which takes up a lot of energy. Therefore, in the immediate situation when life is being threatened, the body shuts down the immune system to conserve energy for running and fighting.

In addition to steroid hormones weakening immune responses, nerve fibers from the brain that infiltrate lymph nodes, the spleen, the thymus, and bone marrow (the central organs of the immune system) also begin to fire and cause the immune system to slow down. Therefore, there are two major physiological systems in the body (the hormonal system and the nervous system) that reduce immune functioning when a person is under a lot of stress. Again, that stress doesn't have to be just from a threat to the person's physical body, but also can result from a threat to his or her psychological or social identity.

Physiological changes caused by the fight-or-flight response described above are highly adaptive for survival in the short run.

If a threat continues for days, weeks, or months (as can occur with chronic psychological stress), however, such changes result in greater susceptibility to disease and health problems. By reducing immune function, stress weakens the body's ability to fight off viruses, bacteria, and fungi (e.g., germs), and may even allow normal cells to degenerate into malignant or cancer cells (which the immune system ordinarily prevents). Furthermore, increases in blood pressure may become permanent, leading to blood vessel damage, stroke, or heart attacks. There is considerable research showing that psychological stress can lead to physical disease and worsen existing health problems.

❧ STRESS AND DISEASE

Psychological stress can induce physiological changes right down to the biochemical level that cause disease.[3] Let's take a look at research that has linked stress with medical illness.

Cancer. As noted earlier, the immune system plays a vital role both in identifying early cancer cells when they are first starting out and also in containing the cancer once it has grown larger and begins to spread and invade other organs. Some scientists say that the immune system is even more important in preventing cancer from spreading than it is in preventing it from starting out.[4] There is an immune cell called a natural killer cell (NK cell) that is particularly important in keeping cancer from spreading, and studies have shown that the stress caused by depression can suppress NK-cell activity to the point that it leads to the spread of cancer. For example, Sandra Levy and colleagues[5] followed seventy-five women with early breast cancer over three months. They examined the relationship between NK-cell activity and psychological status, finding that women who experienced depression and fatigue had lower NK-cell activity. Lower NK-cell activity, in turn, was associated with a greater likelihood of dying from the cancer. These investigators also studied the time to death among thirty-six women with recurrent breast cancer.[6] In that study, women with higher levels of psychological well-being were more likely to live longer than those who were hopeless or sad. This has also been shown among women with cancers of the cervix, uterus, and ovaries, who were more likely to experience a spread of their cancer if they were depressed.[7]

Infections. Because the immune system is so important in preventing viruses and bacteria from infecting the body, it is not surprising that those who have weakened immune systems from stress are more susceptible to infections.[8] Gail Ironson and her colleagues at the University of Miami followed a group of men who tested positive for the human immunodeficiency virus (HIV), finding that anxiety levels were associated with lower NK-cell activity (NK cells also kill viruses, just as they do cancer cells).[9] Other scientists found that stressful life experiences among ninety-three men infected with the AIDS virus were associated with worse health outcomes and with more rapid progression of disease during a three to four-year period.[10]

Stress may increase the risk of becoming infected with other viruses as well, including the virus that causes mononucleosis ("mono"), herpes infections, and even the common cold or flu. For example, Janice Kiecolt-Glaser and her colleagues at the Ohio State University found that family members faced with the stress of caring for a loved one with Alzheimer's disease had decreased immune function that led to a greater likelihood of getting colds or the flu.[11] These investigators also later discovered that older adults experiencing stress were less likely to respond to vaccination for the flu virus.[12] In other words, the immune systems of stressed older adults were not capable of mounting an immune response to the flu vaccine to the same degree as the immune systems of older adults who were not stressed.

Psychological stress can even be shown to affect the immune

function of students and young adults in the prime of health. Kiecolt-Glaser and colleagues found that during periods of high examination stress, second-year medical students did not respond to vaccinations against hepatitis B as well as students in the control group who were not under such stress.[13] Similarly, in one of the largest studies ever done, Sheldon Cohen's group at the University of Pittsburgh inoculated 394 healthy volunteers with a cold virus and compared them to 26 control subjects.[14] Increased psychological stress brought a significant increase in both respiratory infections and colds.

Heart Disease and Stroke. Stress is also associated with an increased likelihood of developing coronary artery disease and high blood pressure. Consider the research done by Anika Rosengren and her colleagues who followed 6,935 middle-aged men for twelve years, examining the relationship between psychological stress and the occurrence of myocardial infarction (heart attack).[15] Among men who rated their stress as low at the beginning of the study, only 6 percent experienced a myocardial infarction, whereas 10 percent of men with high stress ratings experienced heart attacks. This represented a 50 percent increase in risk of having a coronary event, even after taking into account age and other risk factors.

Depression is another strong predictor for the development of coronary artery disease and is associated with worse health outcomes in persons who already have heart disease.[16] Since the 1970s, investigators have been comparing the death rates from heart disease between depressed and non-depressed people. In a review of this research, Glassman and Shapiro report that nine out of ten studies found significantly greater death rates from heart disease among the depressed.[17] Emotions like anger, hostility, impatience, or feeling pressured by time are all strong predictors of coronary heart disease, as the work of Duke University behavioral scientist Redford Williams has shown.[18]

There is also evidence that depression and anxiety increase the risk of stroke. In a study of 2,124 men aged forty-nine to sixty-four, those who suffered from depression, anxiety, and other symptoms of psychological stress were more than three times as likely over a fourteen-year period to have a fatal stroke compared to men who were not experiencing stress. This study was published in the January 2002 issue of *Stroke*, one of the most prestigious neurology research journals in the world, and included an editorial stressing the need for physicians to treat depression and anxiety just like other risk factors for stroke such as high blood pressure or high blood cholesterol. In another thirteen-year study of 1,703 individuals participating in the Baltimore Epidemiologic Catchment Area Survey, also published in *Stroke*, investigators at Johns Hopkins found the risk of stroke was again three times higher among persons who were depressed.[19]

Wound Healing. Stress can even influence the speed at which a wound heals. Because the immune system has such a big role in wound closure and healing after an accident or surgical procedure, anything that disturbs the immune system also interferes with healing. Several studies have now demonstrated this effect. Again, Janice Kiecolt-Glaser's group at the Ohio State University has done some of the most groundbreaking work in this area. In order to test whether stress could impair wound healing, these investigators created a small, uniform wound about the size of a pencil eraser (3.5 millimeters) on the inside cheek of the mouths of experimental subjects. Speed of healing was then measured by serial photographs taken of the wound and its response to application of hydrogen peroxide. First, the team applied the cheek wound to a sample of thirteen stressed family members taking care of loved ones with Alzheimer's disease, and then applied the same wound to a sample of thirteen non-stressed control subjects matched for age and other characteristics. The speed of wound healing was then compared between the two groups. Wound healing took 24 percent longer in the stressed caregiver group compared to the non-stressed controls (approximately nine days longer).[20]

In order to determine whether usual, everyday stresses might have similar effects in young adults, P. T. Marucha and colleagues did the same experiment on eleven dental students, comparing healing responses in the same individuals receiving the wound at two different time points. The first wound was created at the end of summer vacation. The second wound was created three days before the first major exam of the term (a high-stress period). Thus, each student had two identical wounds— one placed during the relaxing summertime and one just before high-stress exams. Amazingly, the wounds took 40 percent longer to heal during the high-stress exam period than during the summer vacation.[21]

Older adults are already predisposed to poor wound healing because of changes in the skin that occur with aging as well as declines in the immune system with age. This leads to reduced wound healing and greater likelihood of complications such as infection and poor wound closure. If stress impairs wound healing even in young persons facing relatively minor stressors, imagine what stress from feeling useless or lacking purpose can do to older adults.

Social Support. Research shows that people who have more supportive and fulfilling interactions with others report less stress in their lives.[22] Given this fact, scientists are now beginning to study whether "social support" reduces the likelihood of stress-induced immune problems and related diseases. What they're finding from such research is relevant to our discussion of purpose and the importance of reaching out to and supporting others.

Among the first of these studies was work done in baboons. Robert Sapolsky's group at Stanford examined the effects of social isolation in a group of seventy African yellow baboons, finding that those with the lowest rank (and greatest isolation) had three times higher cortisol levels than baboons who were more dominant and socially interactive.[23] High cortisol levels, in turn, predicted weaker immune systems and less resistance to disease. Similar effects of stress have been discovered in humans. Psychiatric patients who experience feelings of loneliness are found to have weaker immune systems compared to those who are not lonely.[24] Young, healthy medical students respond less well to vaccinations if they are stressed and have low levels of social support, compared to students who are stressed but have high support.[25] Likewise, stressed older adults with low social support experience greater declines in immune functioning over time compared to those with high social support.[26] Social support has also been shown to ameliorate the stressful effects on immune functioning from caring for loved ones with cancer.[27]

Social support appears to be particularly important in reducing the stress associated with poor outcomes among women with breast cancer. For example, in Sandra Levy's study of seventy-five women with early breast cancer discussed earlier, investigators found that lack of family support was associated with lower NK-cell activity both at the start of the study and after three months of follow-up.[28] They later replicated this finding in another sample of sixty-six women with breast cancer, again discovering greater NK-cell activity among women with higher social support.[29] Given the relationship between lower NK-cell activity and the progression of breast cancer, it's not surprising what David Spiegel's group at Stanford found in a study that I will now describe.

To better understand the effect that increased social support might have on the progression of breast cancer, Spiegel and his colleagues conducted a large clinical trial involving eighty-six women with advanced, widespread breast cancer.[30] Over a period of twelve months, women in the test group participated in weekly supportive group therapy. They would meet together, support each other emotionally, and talk about whatever was bothering them. After ten years, the health outcomes of women receiving support were compared to those of women in the control group (who did not receive support). The women who received support survived nearly twice as long as women in the control group (36.6 months compared to 18.9 months). Several other studies have also found that cancer patients who receive high-quality social support from others survive longer than those who do not.[31]

In addition, social support appears to be an important factor in preventing the negative effects of stress on the heart and on the vessels that supply blood to the heart. After reviewing fourteen studies on the relationship between coronary heart disease, psychological stress, and social support, Daren Greenwood and colleagues concluded that both life stress and social support affect the development of coronary heart disease, but social support had an even greater influence on preventing it than psychological stress had in causing it.[32] For example, Teresa Seeman and S. L. Syme examined the impact of different kinds of social support on coronary disease risk in 119 men and 40 women by measuring degree of coronary atherosclerosis using coronary angiography (injecting dye into the blood vessels of the heart to determine the degree to which they were clogged up with plaque).[33] Investigators discovered that feelings of being loved by others were more important than the actual number of persons in the social network in predicting lower coronary disease risk. They concluded that it was the quality—not the quantity—of social support that mattered most.

Redford Williams and his team at Duke reported similar findings when they studied the effects of social resources on death rates from heart attacks among 1,368 patients with coronary heart disease.[34] Among the most important predictors of survival were being married and having someone to talk to about important problems (a confidante). Subjects who were not married and did not have a confidante experienced a five-year survival rate of 50 percent compared to 82 percent for subjects who were married, had a confidante, or both. Overall, the risk of dying among unmarried subjects without a confidante was over three times greater than that of persons who were married and had a confidante.

These findings suggest that reducing stress, either by increasing social support or some other way, may help to reduce heart disease and bolster the immune system.

❧ WAYS TO REDUCE STRESS

One way to reduce stress is to eliminate the sources of stress. Efforts may be made to control the external environment so that it will be less stressful. In other words, a person may get a less stressful job, win the lottery, inherit a fortune, move to a different neighborhood, take a trip away from family, discover the fountain of youth, become miraculously healed of a chronic health problem, and so on. It would be nice if all stressors could simply be done away with. Most of the time, however, this is not possible. However, it is possible to reduce the amount of stress experienced without changing one's circumstances.

Improve your ability to tolerate stress.

If you are experiencing a lot of stress, then you should do things that will build up resistance against stress and enable you to tolerate it better. For example, get plenty of sleep, rest, and exercise. Be sure to sleep at least eight hours each night and with as few interruptions as possible. If there is noise in the environment (snoring, clanging in the bathroom or kitchen by early risers, barking dogs, singing birds, or honking horns from busy traffic), then sleep with a noisemaker (a machine that provides "white noise" that muffles out other sounds) or sleep with earplugs (the foam variety that expand to fill the ear canal). Exercise is also very important for reducing stress, particularly if done vigorously on a routine basis. Exercise increases the physical body's capacity to withstand stress and can act as a release for negative energy that builds up during the day. I will talk more about exercise in the next chapter.

Do things that are relaxing.

For example, music is relaxing for some people. Certain kinds of classical music are especially effective in this regard, as are instrumentals involving harp or flute music. For Christians, contemporary Christian music played quietly in the background can help to reduce stress. A regular walk or hike around a lake, by a stream, or along the beach can be very relaxing. The sounds of nature have marvelous tranquilizing properties. A funny show on television or radio can also be a great stress buster.

Do something to stay busy.

Develop a hobby, complete a project around the house, do something creative, volunteer—get involved in something that will take your entire concentration. Activity will distract your thoughts away from distressing concerns you might otherwise dwell on. Stress is often a result of focusing attention on something negative and mulling it over and over again. Get yourself thinking about something else to prevent your focusing on distressing thoughts.

Get involved in educational activity.

Education and learning also help to keep the mind occupied so that it does not dwell on unhealthy concerns, worries, or regrets. Learn to play a musical instrument, take a class at a local university, join a reading club, or acquire knowledge that will enable you to make a useful contribution to the world. Renowned educator Virginia C. Gildersleeve said, "Education must make one able to: think straight; have knowledge of the past and a vision for the future; have a skill to do useful service and an urge to act for the well-being of the community. Then America will have the wisdom and courage to match her destiny." In order to stay mentally fit, the retired person needs to keep learning and growing, stay inquisitive and open to new ideas. Writer William Feather said, "An education isn't how much you have committed to memory. It's being able to differentiate between what you know and what you don't. It's knowing where to get information; and knowing how to use it." Armed with experience, retired people can now use it to apply new knowledge in creative ways to benefit themselves and others. When a person is doing that, there's less time to feel anxious or worried about personal problems.

Establish priorities; balance activity with rest.

Establish priorities and set up a time schedule that balances activity with rest. Don't take on too many responsibilities. A retired person should not spend a lot of time feeling behind, harried, and pressured. Choose activities wisely, based on conscious goals, and learn to say "no."

Change your view of the situation.

If you cannot change the situation that is causing stress, then consider changing your *perception* of it. Situations can always be reframed or examined in a different light so that they are less threatening or disturbing. Often, it is quite natural to see things in the worst possible light, viewing a situation pessimistically rather than optimistically. Pessimism involves selecting the negative aspects of a situation and dwelling on those negative aspects, completely ignoring the positive. "Cognitive therapy" is a form of psychotherapy that helps people to view situations in a more balanced and realistic light, since there are always good things and bad things about any circumstance.[35] The key is becoming accustomed to looking for the good things in a situation or the good that could come out of it, rather than focusing on the bad. As the famous psychiatrist Karl Menninger once said, "Attitudes are more important than facts." There is no bad situation that having a positive attitude cannot overcome.

Practice relaxation techniques.

Visualization and progressive relaxation are techniques frequently used by psychologists to help anxious people relax. Visualization involves closing your eyes and imagining you are in a peaceful and calm environment—lying on a warm sandy beach, in a grassy meadow by a stream, or in a forest near a mountain lake. If you choose a beach scene, imagine the waves rolling onto the beach one by one. With each wave that rolls in, say, "I am at peace." Try to synchronize each breath with the waves, taking a slow deep breath inward with each wave and then letting it out with the next wave. If you are imagining a meadow or a forest scene, visualize a leaf at the top of a nearby tree fluttering in the breeze. Imagine the leaf breaking loose from the branch by a gust of wind and then slowly floating to the ground. As the leaf floats slowly downward say, "I am becoming more and more relaxed." Continue to say this with each slow deep breath as the leaf floats farther and farther downward, closer and closer to the ground.

Progressive muscle relaxation is another technique to help loosen up muscles made tense by stress. Start with the face muscles and gradually move down the body to the legs and then to the feet. First, contract the muscles in the brow by lifting the eyelids upward, hold the tension for a count of ten, and then completely relax the brow muscles while saying, "I am letting go of all tension and worry. I am becoming more and more relaxed and at peace." Then move down to the eye muscles, squinting the eyes shut for a count of ten, and then relax them. Next, contract the jaw muscles by clenching the teeth together, then the shoulder muscles by shrugging them, then the arm muscles by flexing the biceps, then the abdominal muscles, the thigh muscles, the calf muscles, all the way down to the feet. Each time, hold the tension for a count of ten and then release it completely, focusing on the warm feeling of relaxation that flows into the muscles as they relax. Again, coordinate breathing so that slow deep breaths are taken in and out, breathing out when the muscle group is relaxed. Therapists often combine visualization and progressive muscle relaxation together, and may give patients an audiotape providing step-by-step instructions.

Seek support and encouragement from others.

Get together with a trusted friend or family member and tell that person about the stressful situation. Let it all out. Tell the friend beforehand what you expect, that what you really need is a listening ear—not advice to solve the problem, but simply someone who will agree to listen and validate. Afterward, go out and do something together with the friend. Go to a movie, a play, a sporting event, shopping, or some other activity that both of you will enjoy and that will get your thoughts completely off the problem.

Try spiritual practices like prayer, worship, and Scripture reading.

Find a quiet place alone and talk to God. Do it silently or do it aloud. Get emotional about it, letting all your feelings and frustrations out. Seek guidance and direction, along with the strength needed for appropriate action. Then, after taking the appropriate action, turn the entire situation over to God.

Also consider praying in a meditative or contemplative manner—called "centering prayer." Catholic theologian Basil Pennington has written extensively about centering prayer as a source of relaxation and peace and as a way to connect more deeply with God.[36] As the prophet Isaiah said, "But those who hope in the LORD will renew their strength. They will soar on wings like eagles; they will run and not grow weary, they will walk and not be faint" (Isaiah 40:31). First, clear your mind of all thoughts. Then focus on a sacred word or phrase and repeat it over and over again in your mind. Other thoughts will intrude, but just try to ignore them. Christians may repeat the phrase, "Lord Jesus Christ, have mercy on me, a sinner," or "God is with me, God is helping me, God is guiding me." Buddhists and Hindus may repeat the mantra, "Om Ah Hum," or simply "Om." In his book *The Relaxation Response*, Herbert Benson emphasizes the same concept. In his work over the years, Benson has shown that such practices can reduce blood pressure, slow the heart rate and breathing, and cause other healthy physiological changes in the body. Other scientists have used meditation to reduce anxiety[37] and to relieve chronic pain.[38]

Besides prayer in solitude, group prayer can also help to reduce stress. Prayer groups are now common in many churches. They add fellowship and social support to the relaxing quality of prayer itself, boosting its effects. Likewise, worshiping and praising God together in song and through the liturgy during a religious service help to release pent-up tensions and get thoughts focused on something positive and uplifting.

Reading, studying, and memorizing Scripture passages help to bathe the mind with healing words that dispel fear and anxiety. For the older Christian contemplating the end of life, the following words of Jesus to Mary and Martha provide hope and a future: "I am the resurrection and the life. He who believes in me will live, even though he dies; and whoever lives and believes in me will never die" (John 11:25–26). Death is not the end. There is life after death, according to Jesus.

Do not dwell in the past.

Much stress comes from thinking about things that have happened long ago and projecting negative outcomes in the future based on the past. Constantly thinking about old hurts, wounds, or failures can lead to increased distress and fear of the future. The words of the apostle Paul are again relevant here: "But one thing I do: Forgetting what is behind and straining toward what is ahead, I press on toward the goal to win the prize for which God has called me" (Philippians 3:13–14). Forget, forgive, and let go. Strive ahead with purpose toward the vision that God has provided. The future is always a blank slate on which anything can be written. Confess mistakes and receive forgiveness, forgive others, and re-establish relationships. Be grateful and thankful for whatever is in the present, and look forward each day to new opportunities and possibilities.

Do good to others.

Booker T. Washington said, "Assistance given to the weak makes the one who gives it strong." Such help is an investment into the lives of others. This investment pays off big by neutralizing feelings of fear and anxiety.

Have a purpose.

Having a purpose or developing a new sense of worthy purpose can help to reduce stress. By giving direction to life, purpose helps to dispel feelings of uselessness that may be fueling worries. Purpose redirects energies into other areas not affected by difficult personal situations causing life stress. Having great goals and throwing your abilities and resources into those goals will distract you from more petty worries and concerns. Having purpose and meaning in life will also enhance self-esteem and self-image, making the self less vulnerable to anxiety. Purpose can generate a hunger for knowledge and creativity that will propel the retired person into new ventures that will neutralize worries over past failures or future concerns.

❧ NOT ALL STRESS IS BAD

A completely stress-free life would eventually become dull, as no new challenges could be faced and overcome. The thrill of success and accomplishment, even little accomplishments, would be gone. Also, stress reveals things about a person that would otherwise not come out. Francis Bacon said, "Prosperity doth best discover vice, but adversity doth best discover virtue." Difficult and stressful situations can teach lessons that otherwise would never be learned, and may help refine character traits that would otherwise not be put to the test.

This point is illustrated by a story recently circulated on the Internet about a group of women in a Bible study who were reviewing the book of Malachi. They came across a verse that read: "He will sit as a refiner and purifier of silver" (Malachi 3:3). The group argued about what the statement meant concerning the character of God and his relationship to people. Someone suggested that one of them go to visit a silversmith and find out what actually goes on during the process of refining silver. One woman offered to go and report to the group what she discovered at their next meeting.

She called around and found a silversmith who was willing to allow her to watch him at work. She didn't mention to him why she was interested but simply said that she needed to know about the process for a project she was working on. She watched the silversmith use a pair of tongs to hold a piece of silver over the fire to heat it up. She asked him about all the details. Why, for example, did he hold the silver so carefully and steadily over the fire? He explained that he had to hold the impure silver at the very center of the fire where the flames were hottest. This was necessary in order to burn away the impurities.

The woman thought to herself quietly. She couldn't imagine God holding someone in a hot spot on purpose. She understood, however, that sometimes people put themselves in the middle of a fire because of mistakes or poor judgments. She thought again about Malachi 3:3, which talked about God as the refiner of silver. Did this mean that God was refining people by supporting and holding them during the fiery trials of life, as the silversmith was doing to get the impurities out of the silver?

She then asked the silversmith if it was necessary for him to sit there in front of the fire the entire time actually holding the silver himself until the process was completed. Why couldn't he just leave the silver there and go about his other business? He answered that it was very important that he stay right there with the silver, and that not only did he have to sit there holding the silver, but he also had to keep his eyes on it the entire time. If the silver remained even a moment too long in the fire, he explained, it would be destroyed. The woman thought for a while, and then asked how he knew when the silver was fully refined. He said to her, "That's easy, ma'am. I know that the refining process is completed when I can see my image in the silver." Indeed, God wants to be able to see his image in his followers, and knows that sometimes it requires fire (stress) to get the impurities out.

❧ CONCLUSION

Stress can either be physical or mental. Among those who have adequate food and shelter, stress is mostly a result of threats to self-identity and relationships with others. Stress causes havoc with a person's peace of mind, well-being, and, as scientists are learning, with physical health as well. No one can or should avoid or escape stress entirely, but many things can be done to manage stress. Chief among the ways of coping with stress is having a worthy purpose and goals that can direct anxieties, tension, and restless energies into activities that will help people grow, give meaning and joy to their lives, and help them make a positive difference in the lives of those around them.

 CHAPTER 9

Live Healthy

"Better keep yourself clean and bright: you are
the window through which you must see the world."
—George Bernard Shaw

WHY DEVOTE An entire chapter to physical health in a book about purpose in retirement? Having good physical health is key to ensuring that people are able to carry out their dreams and goals at this time in life. Being ill, being overweight, being immobile, or having poor endurance makes it more difficult to achieve certain kinds of goals. Regardless of how sick or healthy a person is now, it is always possible to improve health, vigor, and endurance, and thereby optimize physical health. Certainly limitations need to be recognized, but within those limitations it is often amazing the kind of physical development that is possible if it is begun slowly and sustained over time. Maintenance of physical health includes regular doctor visits and screening for medical problems as well as taking medication as prescribed and avoiding negative health habits like smoking and excessive alcohol use. In this chapter I will provide specific recommendations for healthy living in retirement, including those pertaining to diet, exercise, and other health habits.

❧ ROLE OF DIET

Many things about physical health are not under a person's control, such as one's genetic predisposition to certain diseases, susceptibility to health problems with increasing age, and exposure
to dangers in the natural environment (accidents, infectious
germs, air pollution, etc.). In contrast, what people eat—their
diet—is something that is fully under their control. Nevertheless,
at least in America where food is overabundant, many have problems controlling what they eat. The result is that the majority of
Americans are overweight and becoming more so each year.

According to the 1999 National Health and Nutrition Examination Survey, the largest and most reputable study of health
habits in the United States, 61 percent of Americans are overweight or obese.[1] This figure is up from 56 percent in the early
1990s. If obesity is defined as roughly thirty pounds over a
healthy body weight, 27 percent of Americans are considered
obese (almost double the figure of 15 percent in the late 1970s).
African American and Hispanic women are particularly prone
to be overweight, with 44 percent and 37 percent respectively
being at least 20 percent over ideal body weight. Many health
experts say that the problem of overeating is serious and needs
to be tackled as a public health problem in much the same way
as cigarette smoking, drunken driving, and AIDS.

Being overweight is associated with numerous health problems. The health care costs due to obesity in the United States
well exceed $50 billion per year. Diseases associated with being
overweight include diabetes mellitus, endometrial cancer, breast
cancer, colon cancer, gallbladder disease, hypertension, osteoarthritis, and coronary heart disease, to mention just a few.

Healthy Eating

What kinds of food must be eaten in order to obtain the essential nutrients for health and vigor while at the same time keep-

ing weight down or losing weight if necessary? Although activity levels are usually lower during retirement, the body's need for essential nutrients remains the same. Retired people should eat a wide variety of foods while keeping their total calorie intake down. Here are some simple rules.

Foods from the grain products group, along with vegetables and fruits, form the basis for most healthy diets. Choose meals with rice, pasta, potatoes, or bread, along with vegetables and fruit, and lean and low-fat foods from the milk, meat, and bean groups. Limit the addition of fats and sugars during food preparation and at the table. According to the *Dietary Guidelines for Americans* from the U.S. Department of Agriculture,[2] most foods should be chosen from the grain products group (6–11 small to moderate servings per day), the vegetable group (3–5 servings per day), and the fruit group (2–4 servings per day). The guidelines suggest that only moderate amounts of food be eaten from the milk group (2–3 servings per day) and the meat and bean group (2–3 servings per day). Avoid foods that provide few nutrients and are high in fat and sugars. Fruits and vegetables are particularly important for retired persons because they include large amounts of water and fiber that help to regulate bowel and bladder function. Despite this, however, only 13 percent of adults eat the minimum amount of fruits and vegetables needed.

To maintain a certain weight, daily total caloric intake must match calorie expenditures. Typically, sedentary adult women will require 1,600 calories per day and active men will consume 2,800 calories per day. When more calories are consumed than are expended, the extra calories are stored as fat and weight gain occurs. As one grows older, especially past age fifty, metabolic rate begins to slow. This results in the body needing fewer calories, which increases the likelihood of weight gain and fat deposition if eating patterns remain the same as at younger ages.

Tailor Your Diet to Your Medical Profile

Foods should be chosen based on the kinds of physical problems a person has. For example, a diabetic will need to limit simple carbohydrate consumption (sugars) and increase intake of complex carbohydrate foods (fruits and vegetables). A person with high blood pressure will need to limit foods (or soups) that contain high amounts of salt. A person with a history of kidney stones will need to increase fluid intake, especially of citrate-containing drinks like lemonade, and to limit ingestion of foods high in oxalate (like spinach, nuts, and chocolate). Those with constipation need to increase their fiber and fluid intake.

In general, retired people do not drink enough fluids, especially water. With increasing age, thirst and desire to drink fluids declines. This means it is easy to become dehydrated, an especially important problem for those who are taking medication such as diuretics (fluid pills) to lower blood pressure. Thus, it is necessary to consciously maintain an adequate fluid intake. Low-calorie fluids are preferred to keep weight down, and water is the best. Make a habit of drinking at least 6–8 large glasses of fluid daily. Men with enlarged prostates may need to limit their fluid intake in the evening hours and increase intake during the morning. The same is true for women with bladder problems or for those of either gender who take diuretics.

The Role of Vitamins

In general, healthy retired people who are eating a balanced diet from the five food groups (according to the dietary guidelines above) do not require vitamins. All of the vitamins and minerals the body needs are contained in those foods. Adding vitamins will only provide false reassurance that nutritional needs are being met. There is no solid scientific evidence that megavitamin therapy improves health or extends longevity; in fact, taking excessive amounts of vitamins A, D, K, or B-6 can result in toxic levels and health problems. The only exceptions to this rule may be vitamins E and C. Vitamin E at 500–1000 IU twice daily purportedly reduces the risk of heart disease. Vitamin E (500–1000 IU twice daily) and 400 micrograms of B-9 (folate) daily may prevent progressive dementia from Alzheimer's disease. Vitamin C at moderate doses of 500–1000 milligrams twice daily may help to prevent the common cold. All of these reported effects, however, remain highly controversial based on conflicting scientific studies. Furthermore, health problems can develop from taking excessive doses of vitamin E (increased bleeding tendency) and vitamin C (kidney stones or diarrhea). So it is difficult to make a solid recommendation about any vitamin at this point.

For those with certain health conditions, however, extra vitamin and mineral intake may be important. For example, as people age they experience changes in the stomach lining that increase the risk for pernicious anemia, a condition in which the stomach is unable to absorb vitamin B-12. If this condition is present, then one milligram a day of vitamin B-12 taken orally can help overcome the stomach's inability to absorb the vitamin. Persons with a history of kidney stones may benefit from taking 200–400 milligrams daily of vitamin B-6. Those with high cholesterol may benefit from taking 250–500 milligrams of vitamin B-3 (niacinamide) daily. Calcium and vitamin D are necessary for women who are at risk for developing osteoporosis. Persons with chronic illness who are underweight and unable to eat adequate amounts of food from the five food groups may benefit from a daily multivitamin tablet.

Food Supplements
Generally, food supplements add little nutrition to a balanced diet that includes servings from each of the five food groups above. Omega-3 fatty acids (found primarily in fish oil and flaxseeds) may help to improve mood, reduce the pain associated

with arthritis, and preserve cardiovascular health.[3] Fish oil capsules can be taken as a food supplement. Four fish oil capsules taken twice daily are necessary to achieve a minimum recommended dose of 2 grams per day, and up to eight to ten capsules twice daily are needed to reach doses of 5–6 grams per day, as suggested by some experts. An alternative to the capsules (and cheaper, although less palatable) is to take two tablespoons of cod-liver oil daily. Instead of fish oil, omega-3 fatty acids can be obtained by taking two tablespoons (30 cubic centimeters) of flaxseed oil daily, which provides 10 grams of ALA (alpha-linoleic acid, a type of omega-3 fatty acid). Some people also receive arthritis relief by taking glucosamine (1000 milligrams twice daily), although this can get expensive.

For those who are chronically ill, underweight, and malnourished, high-calorie protein-rich drinks such as Ensure™ may improve nutrition but are very expensive and probably don't provide much more than a homemade milkshake.

❧ WEIGHT PROBLEMS IN LATER LIFE

Research shows that, just like all Americans, retired people have problems with being overweight. The best study of weight problems in older adults comes from data collected by the Centers for Disease Control (CDC). Based on the Behavioral Risk Factor Surveillance System (BRFSS) for 1994–97 and from the National Health Interview Survey (NHIS) for 1993–95,[4] information on weight and physical activity was collected in a random sample of over seventy thousand Americans aged fifty-five or older. Overweight was defined as a body mass index (BMI) of greater than or equal to 25 kg/m², where BMI = weight in kilograms ÷ [height in meters]².

Among Americans fifty-five to sixty-four, 63 percent are overweight compared to 59 percent of those sixty-five to seventy-four and 47 percent of those seventy-five or older. The decline in weight problems with increasing age is at least partly due to the fact that physical illness also increases with age and often results in weight loss. The likelihood of being overweight was similar among black men and white men but was higher among black women than white women. This means that nearly two-thirds of persons fifty-five to sixty-four and over half of those over sixty-five are overweight. In order to optimize health, given the negative effects that being overweight have on the physical body during the retirement years, it is imperative to strive for an ideal body weight. Weight charts are available at pharmacies and on the Internet.[5]

Of course, weight is not always under a person's control. Genetic factors often account for weight problems in people who are not overeaters. In such cases, body metabolism slows up as calories are restricted. These people find that no matter how little they eat, they don't lose weight. This can be very frustrating and discouraging. When this occurs, the best way to lose weight is to combine calorie restriction with physical exercise. Exercise helps to increase the body's metabolic rate (even when not exercising), which then increases caloric expenditures.

❧ PHYSICAL EXERCISE

Lack of regular physical exercise is a problem for older adults in the United States. Inactivity becomes more common with increasing age. The prevalence of leisure-time physical inactivity is similar for those fifty-five to sixty-four years old (33 percent) and sixty-five to seventy-four (35 percent), but increases among persons age seventy-five or older—46 percent report no physical activity at all. At least two-thirds of older Americans lead largely sedentary lives,[6] a percentage that is roughly equivalent to the proportion of older adults who are overweight. Lack of physical exercise is not only a problem in retirement, but at any age. Less than 30 percent of the U.S. population exercises at even a moderate level of intensity and even fewer exercise the way they should.[7] Failure to establish an exercise routine during young adulthood and middle age makes it more difficult to establish one after retirement.

Need for Physical Activity

Lack of regular physical exercise has devastating physical consequences for the body. Muscles lose their strength, tendons and ligaments become stiff and inflexible, and as a result, joints become less stable. These physical changes interfere with coordination, make getting around more difficult and painful, and increase the risk of falling. Low levels of physical activity also cause bones to lose calcium and other important minerals, resulting in the development of osteoporosis. Osteoporotic bones are weaker and more fragile and cause chronic pain. Osteoporosis and muscle weakness are important risk factors for falls and fractures in older adults, especially among women.

As an overall prevention strategy, older adults are encouraged to remain active throughout their retirement years to help preserve functional ability and prevent frailty. As aches and pains become more frequent with increasing age, it is natural to respond by reducing activity to avoid discomfort. This tends to reinforce inactivity, which results in further muscle and joint de-conditioning, which makes it harder to be physically active, plunging the person into a vicious downward cycle of increasing debility and dependency. The result is that many retired persons spend a lot of time sitting or lying down, occupied with sedentary activities like watching TV, playing cards, or just sitting around socializing. As noted in chapter 1, this increase in sedentary activity is at least partly a product of a rich and pampered modern society, since throughout most of our history older adults tended to work and to remain physically active until they were too sick to do so. They had no other choice. Today, there are many more options available because of increased leisure time and economic resources that foster a sedentary lifestyle.

Consequences of Physical Inactivity

Physical inactivity in both women and men has been shown to lead to more physical illness, more disability, and more visits to doctors. Physical inactivity is the leading cause of health problems due to coronary heart disease, diabetes mellitus, and hypertension in older women, and regular physical activity has been shown to reduce cardiovascular health problems and increase longevity.[8] Older men, too, experience negative health effects from physical inactivity, and this begins in middle age. In a study of 3,043 middle-aged American men aged twenty-two to seventy-nine, those with lower levels of physical fitness (based on higher sub-maximal exercise test heart rates) were at significantly greater risk of dying of coronary heart disease and other health problems during a twenty-year follow-up.[9] Physical inactivity and lack of exercise result in a loss of both physiological and psychological reserves necessary for optimum functioning and independent living. Studies indicate that medical costs are considerably higher among older persons who are inactive, even after taking into account health problems that limit activity.

Physical inactivity also makes it more difficult to sleep at night. In a ten-year prospective study of over 2,500 men ages thirty to sixty-nine, inactivity was associated with a 42 percent increased likelihood of insomnia and difficulty sleeping.[10] Everyone has restless energy that needs to be expended during the daytime. If that energy is not released, then it may come out as restlessness at night. Vigorous physical activity makes the body physically tired and sends signals to the brain at night that sleep is needed.

Benefits of Regular Exercise

Regular physical exercise is associated with lower rates of many different diseases, including colon cancer, stroke, and back injury. Exercise can also help to prevent or manage heart disease, hypertension, diabetes, osteoporosis, obesity, and emotional disorders such as depression and anxiety. Lack of exercise conveys about the same level of risk seen in persons who smoke cigarettes, have high blood pressure, or have high serum cholesterol. Despite the potential benefits of exercise, fewer than 10 percent of Americans exercise in the way they should (see below).

Just because a person has not been very physically active during retirement doesn't mean this has to continue. Even those who are significantly overweight or physically unfit benefit from starting to exercise. In a sixteen-year study of 2,212 Finnish men and women ages thirty-five to sixty-three, investigators examined the associations between weight, leisure time physical activity, perceived physical fitness, and risk of mortality.[11] Although increased body weight did not predict greater mortality from cardiovascular disease or other health problems, physical fitness and leisure time physical activity did. An increase in physical activity reduced the mortality risk for both obese and non-obese subjects, and for both physically fit and physically unfit subjects alike.

With proper training, physically ill older adults can safely learn to exercise and reduce their weight. A study by Anita L. Stewart and her colleagues examined the effectiveness of a physical activity promotion program on physical activity levels of older adults.[12] Participants chose activities to become involved in that took into account their health, preferences, and abilities. The program also offered information on ways to exercise safely, to motivate themselves, to overcome barriers, and to develop a balanced exercise and rest regimen. All participants in this one-year randomized controlled trial were physically underactive seniors who were patients at a multispecialty medical clinic. One hundred sixty-four subjects aged sixty-five to ninety (two-thirds female) completed the study. Subjects who received the physical activity program increased their expenditure of calories by 687 calories a week, compared to virtually no change in calorie expenditure by members of the control group. Overweight persons were especially likely to benefit from this program, which was as effective for women, older adults (75+), and those who did not exercise at baseline, as for men, younger elders, and those who were already exercising at the start of the study. The investigators concluded that individually tailored programs that encourage lifestyle changes among older adults are effective in both increasing exercise and calorie expenditure.

Best Kind of Exercise

The best kind of exercise is the one that a person will stick to and won't give up on when it starts getting painful, boring, or inconvenient. In other words, the best exercise is one that will be done day in and day out on a regular basis. Exercise needs to become a daily habit just like eating and sleeping. The kind of exercise typically recommended by doctors is the kind that uses large muscle groups for twenty to thirty minutes (running, walking, swimming, or bicycling) at least three days a week and is performed at 60 percent or greater of a person's maximum cardio-respiratory capacity.[13] Again, fewer than 10 percent of Americans exercise regularly in this manner.

Starting an Exercise Regimen

Anyone beginning to exercise should start slowly and easily. If you have not exercised in a long time, consult a doctor or a physical therapist to develop an exercise plan. Such a plan should include learning to stretch muscles before beginning to exercise, developing an exercise schedule of gradually increasing duration and intensity, and learning about the warning signs that suggest you might be overdoing it. At least ten minutes of warmup and ten minutes of cool-down should be included as part of the exercise program.

Find a time to exercise during the day that will not interrupt other activities. Some people exercise twenty to thirty minutes immediately before breakfast or dinner. It is probably not a good idea to exercise soon after meals, since part of your blood volume will be diverted to the stomach for digestion. Those who have circulatory problems or who are taking certain medications that slow the heart or reduce blood pressure will be at increased risk for complications if they exercise after a heavy meal. Also, avoid exercising immediately before retiring at night, since it may interfere with your ability to fall asleep.

Combining Exercise with Spiritual Activity

Exercise can be combined with spiritual activity, making both more fulfilling and enjoyable. This also increases the likelihood that the activities will be carried out regularly. An example is "prayer walking," described by Janet McHenry in her book *Prayer Walk*.[14] McHenry defines prayer walking as "Spending time with God in adoration and intercession as I walk the streets and highways of my community."[15] This can be done as a solitary activity, as McHenry describes above, or as a group activity. Spiritual growth and physical fitness all at the same time—what a deal!

❧ AVOID UNHEALTHY HABITS

Cigarette or cigar smoking, pipe smoking, and chewing tobacco should be avoided entirely, given their association with mouth and lung cancer, high blood pressure, and coronary heart disease. Since over 25 percent of the population smokes regularly, tobacco is the single most preventable cause of death and disease in the United States.[16] Excessive alcohol use can also lead to multiple health problems, including cirrhosis of the liver, high blood pressure, stomach ulcers, and esophageal problems, not to mention the short-term and long-term effects on memory, concentration, and motor coordination. How much alcohol is excessive for an older adult? Heavy drinking is defined as more than two drinks a day or occasional consumption of five drinks or more (a drink is defined as twelve ounces of beer, five ounces of wine, or one ounce of liquor). Blood-alcohol levels increase with increasing age due to lower levels of body water and reduced lean muscle mass. As a result, a single drink of alcohol will result in a 20 percent higher blood-alcohol level at age sixty-five than at age thirty.

Tranquilizers and sedatives (anti-anxiety drugs and sleeping pills) may also be used in excessive amounts during the retirement years. This is a problem particular among older women. Bear in mind, however, that there are many valid reasons for taking these medications, including the treatment of anxiety disorders and properly diagnosed sleep disorders. Nevertheless, sedatives have the potential for misuse and abuse. These medications are associated with memory problems, coordination difficulties, and falls, so they can have serious side effects and negative health consequences just as alcohol does. Excessive alcohol and sedative use is more common among retired persons whose lives lack purpose and meaning, who feel bored or believe their lives are useless, and those who have a lot of free leisure time on their hands. Those who are striving and seeking to fulfill a worthy purpose have less need and less time to abuse such substances.[17]

❧ CONCLUSION

Living healthy in retirement will help to maintain physical health and prevent disease that threatens the quality of life. While health is not required for purpose and power in retirement, it sure helps. Healthy living involves eating nutritious, low-calorie foods, minimizing intake of sweets and fat, striving to attain and maintain an ideal body weight, exercising regularly, and avoiding alcohol and drugs. "Hey," one might say, "you're taking away all the fun things in life and replacing them with activity that requires effort and sweat!" Good health requires sacrifice and discipline—there's no way around that. But it's worth it. Is there anything else in life that rivals feeling good physically, having plenty of energy, being mentally sharp, resting well at night, and being capable of charting the course of your own life, independent and self-sufficient? Yes, it's definitely worth the effort.

CHAPTER 10

Steps to Purpose
and Power in Retirement

*"You will be made rich in every way
so that you can be generous on every occasion."* —2 *Corinthians* 9:11

O s GUINNESS SAID, "A sense of purpose and fulfillment is the single strongest issue flowing out of the quest for meaning.... [N]othing better illuminates the entire journey of life and faith, and in particular the special challenge of finishing well, than the issue of purpose." It is indeed a special challenge—"finishing well." How is that possible without purpose? How can the Olympic runner cross the finish line if he or she does not know where the finish line is? Thomas Carlyle said it this way: "The man without purpose is like a ship without a rudder—a waif, a nothing, a no-man." Dostoevsky described in *The Brothers Karamazov* what happens to a person when he or she comes to doubt the purpose of life. He said, "For the secret of man's being is not only to live ... but deliver something definite. Without a firm notion of what he is living for, man will not accept life and will rather destroy himself than remain on earth." This indeed has been the choice of many philosophers throughout the ages—lacking a sense of purpose and meaning, they have struggled in their old age.

Any major transition or change will challenge one's sense of meaning and purpose. And there are plenty of transitions with the event of retirement and afterward. As these transitions occur, the will to live sometimes becomes less certain, the mission in life less clear. This is normal and natural, and propels a person to reach out and discover new purpose. Below are ten concrete steps that, if taken seriously, will help achieve a purpose-filled retirement.

1. **Do a life review.** Think about why you are alive at this time and in this place. In a speech he gave in Berlin in 1932, Albert Einstein said, "Our situation on this earth seems strange. Every one of us appears here involuntarily and uninvited for a short stay, without knowing the whys and the wherefore." Is it really not possible to know the "whys and the wherefore" during this lifetime? Is it truly such a mystery? Are there not clues all around us? Are those clues not trying to force themselves into our awareness, and do not many people try to push them away using their intellect as a battering ram?

   Think back over the years. Were your successes real and worth the effort? Think about what gave your life purpose and meaning during those earlier days. Then consider what purpose your life might serve starting now—in your remaining years on this earth, the precious time that is now left. Struggle with this for a while. Begin to review and examine your life. Don't ignore or suppress these crucial questions as most people do.

2. **Take a spiritual inventory.** How important have spiritual matters been in your life? If they have been important in the past, seek to nourish them in the present. If they have not been very important, then start thinking about them more. Os Guinness has written a wonderful book for the person who is seeking the truth about the spiritual meaning of life called *The Long Journey Home*. It will help you with your search. A strong spiritual life can make the steps

that follow a lot easier. Be prepared to make an effort—no good thing or lasting change comes without that. With time, however, your effort will become self-sustaining.

3. **Decide on a worthy purpose.** Consider your strengths and abilities. How can those abilities be used to affect the lives of others in a positive way? Are there goals you could set that would make your life more meaningful? Remember that nothing gives power and energy like a worthy purpose, and a worthy purpose always has something to do with being generous with time, money, and love. The Greek philosopher Sophocles said, "To be doing good is man's most glorious task." Decide what to accomplish during these retirement years and commit to it. Write it down. Then share it with a friend or loved one and ask him or her to help keep you on track.

4. **Move ahead to fulfill that purpose.** After doing a life review, taking a spiritual inventory, and deciding on a worthy purpose, begin to move ahead in fulfilling that purpose. Start using your talents and gifts, no matter how small or large, to propel yourself ahead towards the goals you have set. While it is never too late to get going, "going" has to start sometime. Even if there is a possibility that the goals you set were wrong, start moving anyway—take a chance. Nothing is ever absolutely certain. If your goals are wrong ones, trust that life will provide warnings and plenty of time to change direction—if you stay alert. Something will eventually feel "right" and will "fit" with your personality and circumstances. Remember that the past is the past. Learn from it and leave it behind. Start moving ahead.

5. **Slowly increase your level of involvement.** Start moving ahead slowly and cautiously at first, especially if investing

time, money, or other resources into a new endeavor. Don't make a big commitment that you can't follow through, or that might later need to be abandoned because it doesn't fit your abilities and talents. Gradually increase your involvement as you learn more about what the activity will entail. For example, if you decide to volunteer to help a home-bound needy older person, start with a few hours each week. Continue at this level until it becomes clear to you that the activity is a good use of your time and that it will fulfill the purpose and goals you have set. As you become more and more certain that the activity is right for you and that there are additional needs to be met, increase your involvement as your schedule and resources allow. If necessary, recruit others to help spread out the work and provide companionship.

6. **Develop a time schedule and monitor it.** Carefully review how your day is spent. Develop a list of all your activities. Decide which of your activities are really important and which are not. Be ruthless in eliminating activities that do not relate to goals you have set. Many things people do aren't really necessary and tend to crowd out activities that are truly meaningful. Be shrewd in identifying unnecessary activities that lead neither to pleasure nor to purpose. Also, don't allow others to fill up or determine your schedule, but carefully and consciously plot it out yourself. At the same time, keep a schedule that is flexible, since human needs don't always follow a time schedule. Don't over-commit to activities, even to those that support your retirement goals, since this can quickly lead to burnout. Burnout is where the stress involved in an activity becomes intolerable and makes the activity burdensome and unpleasant. While it is important to "count the cost" and to realize that achieving any worthy goal requires effort and perseverance,

overcommitting to too many activities will exhaust your time and resources and is counterproductive.

7. **Take time to rejuvenate and relax.** During youth, most of us overdo it in play and recreation. During middle age, most of us overdo it in work as we strive to establish and maintain successful careers. During retirement, things should be different. After two-thirds of a lifetime of experience, retirement should be a <u>time of balance</u>. Balance in work and play. Enjoy the fruits of your labor—but don't fall into the trap of making the purpose of retirement the enjoyment of that fruit. As emphasized throughout this book, leisure, consumption, and pleasure will take a person only so far. <u>There is a higher, greater purpose to life.</u> Part of that purpose, however, includes rest and relaxation—which are required to reach important goals that require a sustained effort. Take time to pray, to reconnect with God, and to allow God's rest, peace, and strength to flow into you. Any continuous effort without a break will drain energy and sap motivation. It will make you feel grumpy and less able to love and care for others. Individuals differ in the amount of rest they require for rejuvenation. When boredom sets in, however, that is a clear sign that you have rested enough.

8. **Pay attention to your health.** Physical health will set limits on the kind of goals that can be achieved during retirement. Maintaining physical health will keep more options open, and neglecting your body will restrict those options. This does not mean that those who are sick cannot have purpose and serve in meaningful ways. However, it is one thing to become ill through no fault of your own, and something totally different to get sick because of neglect or lack of discipline. For that reason, it is important to get

regular medical checkups, follow your doctor's advice, take medications as prescribed, exercise, eat a healthy diet, get plenty of sleep, reach and maintain an ideal body weight, and avoid behaviors that destroy health such as smoking cigarettes or excessive alcohol use. Commit yourself to a healthy lifestyle.

9. **Identify someone to model.** Identify a role model, and learn about that person's life. Learn how and why he (or she) did what he did. Find someone who achieved a worthy goal that is similar to the one you've chosen for your retirement years—someone who started out with similar resources. Examples of role models might include: Mother Teresa, St. John of God, Sir John Templeton, Norman Vincent Peale, Ruth S. Peale, Rosalyn Carter, Jimmy Carter, Mahatma Gandhi, Desmond Tutu, or Henri Nouwen.

Consider the lives of others who have made significant contributions late in their lives. For example, at the age of seventy-two, Galileo wrote *Dialoghi Delle Nuove Scienze*, which summarized much of his early work on the principles of mechanics. In his late seventies, Alexander Humboldt wrote the initial two volumes of *Kosmos* (his famous text on planetary cosmology) and completed two more volumes in his late eighties. Sigmund Freud did most of his work on psychoanalysis between the ages of sixty-seven and eighty-two. At the age of seventy-eight, Benjamin Franklin invented the bifocal. For those with purpose, age is no limitation. Read about the lives of people who demonstrate this quality.

10. **Remember, everyone has a calling.** Os Guinness defines "calling" as "simply that God calls us to himself so decisively that everything we are, everything we do, and everything we have is invested with the special devotion and

dynamism lived out as a response to his summons and service." There is a special mission for every person, a mission that only that person has the unique combination of talents and abilities and circumstances to carry out. It doesn't matter whether the person is rich or poor, smart or dumb, healthy or sick. God created each person completely unique, just as one person's fingerprint is different from the fingerprint of any other person who has ever lived. In whatever circumstance you might find yourself—no matter how challenging—it is *there* that you have been called to make a difference. Today is a critical time in history with great human need at every turn. Don't ignore the divine calling to meet that need. If restlessness, boredom, or feelings of uselessness set in, then these feelings are signals that there is indeed more to life. The key to experiencing and enjoying that *more* is identifying and fulfilling God's purpose for your life.

Conclusion

*"When looking back, usually I'm more sorry
for the things I didn't do than for the things
I shouldn't have done."* —Malcolm S. Forbes

S OCIAL SCIENTISTS have identified retirement as a stressful event for some. Leaving the workforce can significantly challenge a person in numerous ways—financially, socially, and emotionally. Work serves many psychological needs, including structured activity within a regular time frame and a sense of purpose and meaning. Energy is directed into intellectual, creative, and/or physical tasks that offer satisfaction when they are completed. All of that ends with retirement, and for some, can precipitate an identity crisis.

The key to a vibrant, satisfying, and meaningful retirement is to find new purpose—a goal toward which to strive that gives meaning, satisfaction, and a sense of reward. Finding purpose is more urgent than ever during the retirement years, when the search for purpose becomes one of the deepest of human longings. American society today offers resources and opportunities for choice and change in almost everything we do. However, among the great civilizations in human history, this is the first to have no generally agreed upon answer to the question: "What is the purpose of life?" As Os Guinness says, "too much to live with and too little to live for."

To experience real power during retirement, the purpose and goals chosen must be worthy ones that direct our attention and energy outside of our own self-centered lives. Goals are particularly worthwhile when they are associated with helping those in need—providing support and care for the lonely, reaching out to those in pain, giving time and resources and sacrificing personal comfort in order to bring comfort to others. For most people, getting the focus off our own world and onto the world of others is a hard step to take. It is a step that I struggle with every day, since it goes against my natural instinct that tempts me to focus on my own obsessive desires, worries, and concerns. However, to the feeble extent that I've been able to take that step, I've tasted the results—the overpowering sense that I am accomplishing the purpose for which I was created. I'm convinced that it works this way whether a person is sick or healthy. It's a law imbedded within the universe. A person must truly lose his life before he can find it—there is really no other pathway to it.

For most of us, however, it will take a great deal of effort, self-discipline, and sacrifice to get oriented and moving toward that worthy target—almost like a Titan missile that has to expend tremendous energy to get off the earth and move toward outer space, while the earth holds it tightly by gravity. Old habits of self-centeredness hold us fast like gravity to material pleasures and securities. After the boost of energy required for change, we will be propelled ahead with purpose that produces greater and greater returns on that initial investment of energy, with less and less effort. No doubt, occasional bursts of effort will be necessary to keep us on track, just as the small guide rockets on the Titan missile keep it moving toward its destination. For humans, spiritual guide rockets can provide power and direction for change.

Our initial resistance, though, is hard to overcome. We are afraid to take the leap; it is difficult to have enough trust or faith to break free from the "what ifs" that descend and quickly

paralyze us. What if you give your time, talents, and money—
and don't get anything out of it? What if you get sick and need
the resources you have given away? What if you lose power,
influence, and control over others? These are false anxieties and
concerns. Those who give freely of themselves to others without
expectation of reward always get back much more than they
give—it is an eternal law that cannot be altered or revoked.
Consider what the great holy men, prophets, and poets throughout the ages have said:

+ Moses (circa 1400 B.C.):
  "Do not seek revenge or bear a grudge against one of your
  people, but love your neighbor as yourself." —Leviticus
  19:18

+ Krishna (900 B.C.):
  "One who engages in full devotional service [to others],
  who does not fall down under any circumstance, at once
  transcends the modes of material nature and thus comes
  to the level of Brahman." —Bhagavad-Gita 14:26[1]

+ Gautama Buddha (563–483 B.C.):
  "Consider others as yourself." —Dhammapada 10:1

+ Confucius (551–479 B.C.):
  "He who wishes to secure the good of others has already
  secured his own."[2]

+ Lucius Annaeus Seneca (4 B.C.–A.D. 65):
  "Live for thy neighbor if thou wouldst live for thy self."

+ Jesus of Nazareth (A.D. 0–32):
  "Love your neighbor as yourself." —Matthew 19:19 and

"Do to others as you would have them do to you."
—Luke 6:31

✦ Muhammad (A.D. 570–632):
"Whatever good ye give, shall be rendered back to you, and
ye shall not be dealt with unjustly." —Sura 2:272

✦ Ralph Waldo Emerson (A.D. 1803–1882):
"If you love and serve men, you cannot by any hiding or
stratagem escape the remuneration. Secret retributions are
always restoring the level, when disturbed, of the Divine
justice. It is impossible to tilt the beam. All the tyrants and
proprietors and monopolists of the world in vain set their
shoulders to heave the bar. Settles forevermore the pon-
derous equator to its line, and man and mote and star and
sun must range within it, or be pulverized by the recoil."

No major religion, philosophy, or belief system has ever
taught that selfishness brings happiness and health—except perhaps one: the theory of natural selection. This theory argues
that only the fittest survive. In other words, organisms are more
likely to live on and propagate their species if they are aggressively competitive for the resources needed to survive. Giving
resources to others or loving your enemies instead of destroying
them is ridiculous, and likely to result in your own annihilation
and extinction.

While the theory of natural selection probably works pretty
well in the plant and animal kingdoms, it is a different story
with humans. In our species, it may be that it is *only* when our
natural animal instinct toward selfishness is overcome that we
can truly survive and live a life that is emotionally and spiritually fulfilling and meaningful on that "higher plane" of existence
that perhaps gives us a glimpse of the eternity to come.

The search for purpose in retirement may be the most important task that many of us have remaining. Finding it could be the key to empowering and transforming these precious years, crowning one's life with significance and meaning regardless of individual circumstances. I know that I've just barely started on the path. I wish you success and Godspeed on this journey and hope to see you on the way.

✥ Notes

INTRODUCTION

1. Dora L. Costa, *The Evolution of Retirement: An American Economic History, 1880–1990* (Chicago: University of Chicago Press, 1998), 7.

2. Ibid., 192.

3. Kenneth G. Manton and James W. Vaupel, "Survival after the Age of 80 in the United States, Sweden, France, England, and Japan," *New England Journal of Medicine* 333 (1995): 1232–35.

4. Costa, *Evolution of Retirement*, 193.

5. Bureau of the Census, *Projections of the Total Resident Population by 5-Year Age Groups, and Sex with Special Age Categories: Middle Series, 1999 to 2100;* available from: http://www.census.gov/population/projections/nation/summary/np-t3-f.pdf (Washington, D.C., 2001).

CHAPTER 1: THE HISTORY OF RETIREMENT

1. Marc Freedman, *Prime Time: How Baby Boomers Will Revolutionize Retirement and Transform America* (New York: Public Affairs Publishers, 1999), 32–74.

2. William Graebner, *The History of Retirement: The Meaning and Function of an American Institution, 1885–1978* (New Haven: Yale University Press, 1980), 10–11.

3. Andrew W. Achenbaum, *Old Age in the New Land: The American Experience Since 1790* (Baltimore: Johns Hopkins University Press, 1978).

4. Ibid.

5. Freedman, *Prime Time*, 41.

6. David H. Fischer, *Growing Old in America* (New York: Oxford University Press, 1977).

7. Thomas R. Cole, "Putting Off the Old: Middle-class Morality, Antebellum Protestantism, and the Origins of Ageism," *Old Age in a Bureaucratic Society,*

ed. D. D. VanTassel and P. N. Sterans (Westport, Conn.: Greenwood Press, 1986).

8. Robert W. Fogel, *Without Consent or Contract: The Rise and Fall of American Slavery* (New York: Norton, 1989).

9. Dora L. Costa, *The Evolution of Retirement: An American Economic History, 1880–1990* (Chicago: University of Chicago Press, 1998), 12.

10. D. K. Brundage, "The Incidence of Illness among Wage Earning Adults," *Journal of Industrial Hygiene* 12 (December 1930): 385–86.

11. William Osler, "The Fixed Period," *Aequanimitas: With Other Addresses to Medical Students, Nurses and Practitioners of Medicine* (Philadelphia, 1910), 391–411.

12. Costa, *Evolution of Retirement*, 106.

13. Carole Haber and B. Gratton, *Old Age and the Search for Security: An American Social History* (Indianapolis: Indiana University Press, 1994).

14. Costa, *Evolution of Retirement*, 17.

15. Ibid., 16.

16. Ibid., 17.

17. Graebner, *History of Retirement*, 186.

18. Ibid., 15.

19. Costa, *Evolution of Retirement*, 17.

20. Freedman, *Prime Time*, 49.

21. Costa, *Evolution of Retirement*, 17.

22. Robert K. Burns, "Economic Aspects of Aging and Retirement," *American Journal of Sociology* 59 (January 1954): 389.

23. Graebner, *History of Retirement*, 228.

24. Freedman, *Prime Time*, 50.

25. Eugene Staley, ed., *Creating an Industrial Civilization: A Report on the Corning Conference, 17–19 May 1951* (Corning, N.Y.: American Council of Learned Societies and the Corning Glass Works, 1952), 63–64.

26. Graebner, *History of Retirement*, 231.

27. Ibid., 234–35.

28. "A Place in the Sun," *Time* (August 3, 1962).

29. Freedman, *Prime Time*, 71.

30. Costa, *Evolution of Retirement*, 173.

31. Matt Moore and John C. Goodman, *Straight Talk about the Social Security Trust Fund*, brief analysis #366 prepared for the National Center for Policy Analysis, 10 August 2001; available from http://www.ncpa.org/pub/ba/ba366/.

32. United Nations, Population Division, Department of Economic and Social Affairs, *Population Aging–1999*, publication ST/ESA/SER.A/179 (1999).

33. Board of Trustees of the Federal Old-Age and Survivors Insurance and Disability Trust Funds, 1996.

34. Costa, *Evolution of Retirement*, 181.

CHAPTER 2: MYTHS OF RETIREMENT

1. Patricia Drentea, "The Best or Worst Years of Our Lives? The Effect of Retirement and Activity Characteristics on Well-being," *Dissertation Abstracts International*, vol. 60, no. 5-A (1999): 1771.

2. David J. Ekerdt, R. Bosse, and S. Levkoff, "An Empirical Test for Phases of Retirement: Findings from the Normative Aging Study," *Journal of Gerontology* 40, no. 1 (1985): 95–101.

3. John W. Rowe and Robert L. Kahn, *Successful Aging* (New York: Random House, 1999).

4. Barbara Vinick and David J. Ekerdt, "Retirement and the Family," *Generations* 13, no. 2 (1989): 53–56.

5. Scott M. Myers and Alan Booth, "Men's Retirement and Marital Quality," *Journal of Family Issues* 17, no. 3 (1996): 336–57.

6. Thomas Johnston, "Retirement: What Happens to the Marriage?" *Issues in Mental Health Nursing* 11, no. 4 (1990): 347–59.

7. Gary R. Lee and Constance L. Shehan, "Retirement and Marital Satisfaction," *Journals of Gerontology* 44, no. 6 (1989): 226–30.

8. Terry L. Gall, D. R. Evans, and J. Howard, "The Retirement Adjustment Process: Changes in the Well-being of Male Retirees across Time," *Journals of Gerontology* 52B, no. 3 (1997): 110–17.

9. Helen Achat, I. Kawachi, A. Spiro 3rd, D. A. DeMolles, and D. Sparrow, "Optimism and Depression as Predictors of Physical and Mental Health Functioning: The Normative Aging Study," *Annals of Behavioral Medicine* 22, no. 2 (2000): 127–30.

10. Harold G. Koenig, J. N. Kvale, and C. Ferrel, "Religion and Well-being in Later Life," *The Gerontologist* 28 (1988): 18–28.

11. Neal Krause, "Social Support," *Handbook of Aging and the Social Sciences,*

5th ed., ed. Robert H. Binstock and Linda K. George (San Diego, Calif.: Academic Press, 2001), 272–94.

12. Elizabeth Midlarsky and Eva Kahana, *Altruism in Later Life* (Thousand Oaks, Calif.: Sage Publications, 1994).

13. David G. Myers, *The Pursuit of Happiness* (New York: William Morrow, 1993).

14. Report, Center on Budget and Policy Priorities, 10 October 2000; available from www.cbpp.org/9-26-00pov.htm.

15. U. S. Social Security Administration, *Social Security Today* 5, no. 6 (November-December 2000): 1; available from http://www.ssa.gov/pubs/oonov-decem.pdf.

16. "In 'Over Our Heads': Credit Card Company Write-offs Set to Hit a Record High, an S&P Report Finds," *CNN/Money*, 26 December 2001; available from http://money.cnn.com/2001/12/26/debt/q_credit/index.htm.

17. Rowe and Kahn, *Successful Aging*.

18. Edward McAuley, Bryan Blissmer, David X. Marquez, Gerald J. Jerome, Arthur F. Kramer, and Jeffrey Katula, "Social Relations, Physical Activity and Well-being in Older Adults," *Preventive Medicine* 31 (2000): 608–17.

19. William S. Shaw, T. L. Patterson, S. Semple, and I. Grant, "Health and Well-being in Retirement: A Summary of Theories and Their Implications," *Handbook of Clinical Geropsychology*, ed. M. Hersen and V. B. Van Hasselt (New York: Plenum Press, 1998), 383–409.

20. Jersey L. Liang, L. Dworkin, E. Kahana, and F. Maziau, "Social Integration and Morale: A Re-examination," *Journal of Gerontology* 35 (1980): 746–57.

21. John C. Cavanaugh, "Friendships and Social Networks among Older People," *Clinical Geropsychology*, ed. Inger Hilde Nordhus, Gary R. Vanden-Bos et al. (Washington, D.C.: American Psychological Association, 1998), 137–40.

22. Robert E. Harlow and Nancy Cantor, "Still Participating After All These Years: A Study of Life Task Participation in Later Life," *Journal of Personality & Social Psychology* 71, no. 6 (1996): 1235–49.

23. Darcy Clay Siebert, E. J. Mutran, and D. C. Reitzes, "Friendship and Social Support: The Importance of Role Identity to Aging Adults," *Social Work* 44, no. 6 (1999): 522–33.

24. Dan G. Blazer, "Social Support and Mortality in an Elderly Community Population," *American Journal of Epidemiology* 115, no. 5 (1982): 684–94.

25. James S. House, K. R. Landis, and D. Umberson, "Social Relationships and Health," *Science* 241, no. 4865 (1988): 540–45.

26. Dora L. Costa, *The Evolution of Retirement: An American Economic History, 1880–1990* (Chicago: University of Chicago Press, 1998).

27. John P. Robinson and Gordon Godby, *Time for Life: Surprising Ways That Americans Use Their Time* (University Park, Pa.: Pennsylvania State University Press, 1999), 136–54.

28. Neal Krause, A. R. Herzog, and E. Baker, "Providing Support to Others and Well-being in Later Life," *Journal of Gerontology* 47, no. 5 (1992): 300–11.

29. S. Stein, M. W. Linn, and E. M. Stein, "The Relationship of Self-help Networks to Physical and Psychosocial Functioning," *Journal of the American Geriatrics Society* 30, no. 12 (1982): 764–68.

30. Elizabeth Mutran and Donald C. Reitzes, "Intergenerational Support Activities and Well-being among the Elderly: A Convergence of Exchange and Symbolic Interaction Perspectives," *American Sociological Review* 49, no. 1 (February 1984): 117–30.

31. Erdman B. Palmore, *The Facts on Aging Quiz*, 2nd ed. (New York: Springer Publishing Co., 1998), 10, 12.

32. Ibid., 11.

33. *The New Non-Profit Almanac: Facts and Figures on the Independent Sector, 2001* (Washington, D.C.: The Independent Sector, 2001); available from http://www.indepsec.org/.

34. Harold G. Koenig, Michael E. McCullough, and David B. Larson, *Handbook of Religion and Health* (New York: Oxford University Press, 2001).

35. *New Non-Profit Almanac 2001*.

36. Palmore, *Facts on Aging Quiz*, 24.

37. Louis Harris and Associates, *Aging in the Eighties* (Washington, D.C.: National Council on the Aging, 1981).

38. See http://www.civicventures.org/site/links/links.html#Anchor-Service-11481.

39. Kenneth G. Manton, L. Corder, and E. Stallard, "Chronic Disability Trends in Elderly United States Populations: 1982–1994," *Proceedings of the National Academy of Sciences of the United States of America* 94, no. 6 (1997): 2593–98.

40. Kenneth G. Manton and X. Gu, "Changes in the Prevalence of Chronic Disability in the United States: Black and Nonblack Population above

Age 65 from 1982 to 1999," *Proceedings of the National Academy of Sciences of the United States of America* 98, no. 11 (2001): 6354–59.

41. Barry Gurland, "Psychopathology," *The Encyclopedia of Aging*, ed. G. Maddox (New York: Springer Publishing Co., 1995).

42. Elizabeth Midlarsky and Eva Kahana, *Altruism in Later Life* (Thousand Oaks, Calif.: Sage Publications, 1994).

43. Michael D. Lemonick and Alice P. Mankato, "The Nun Study: How One Scientist and 678 Sisters Are Helping to Unlock the Secrets of Alzheimer's," *Time*/(May 14, 2001): 54–64.

44. Marc Freedman, *Prime Time: How Baby Boomers Will Revolutionize Retirement and Transform America* (New York: Public Affairs Publishers, 1999), 49.

45. Center on Budget and Policy Priorities, October 10, 2000 report; available from www.cbpp.org/9-26-00pov.htm.

46. Ibid.

47. *New Non-Profit Almanac 2001*.

Chapter 3: Retirement Can Be Deadly

1. Marc Freedman, *Prime Time: How Baby Boomers Will Revolutionize Retirement and Transform America* (New York: Public Affairs Publishers, 1999), 12

2. R. G. Woodbury, "Early Retirement in the United States," Metropolitan Insurance Companies Statistical Bulletin 80, no. 3 (1999): 2–7.

3. Department of Health and Human Services, *Healthy People 2010 (January 2000)*, vol. 1 (Washington, D.C.), 10.

4. Robert N. Butler, *Why Survive? Growing Old in America* (New York: Harper & Row, 1975).

5. Ibid., 72.

6. Peter G. Peterson, *Gray Dawn: How the Age Wave Will Transform America—and the World* (New York: Times Books, 1999).

7. Maurice Silverman, "Psychological and Social Aspects of Psychiatric Disorders in the Aged," *Journal of Mental Science* 99 (1953): 257–64.

8. Edrita G. Fried, "Attitudes of the Older Population Groups toward Activity and Inactivity," *Journal of Gerontology* (1949): 4, 141–51.

9. Virginia E. Richardson and Keith M. Kilty, "Adjustment to Retirement: Continuity vs. Discontinuity, "*International Journal of Aging and Human Development* 33, no. 2 (1991): 151–69.

10. Sylvie Lapierre, J. Pronovost, M. Dube, and I. Delisle, "Risk Factors Associated with Suicide in Elderly Persons Living in the Community," *Canada's Mental Health* 40, no. 3 (1992): 8–12.

11. V. Jayashree and T. Rao, "Effects of Work Status on Adjustment and the Life Satisfaction of the Elderly," *Indian Journal of Clinical Psychology* 18, no. 2 (1991): 41–44.

12. Michal E. Mor-Barak, A. E. Scharlach, L. Birba, and J. Sokolov, "Employment, Social Networks, and Health in the Retirement Years," *International Journal of Aging & Human Development* 35, no. 2 (1992): 145–59.

13. Raymond Bosse, C. Aldwin, M. Levenson, K. Workman-Daniels, and D. Ekerdt, "Differences in Social Support among Retirees and Workers: Findings from the Normative Aging Study," *Psychology and Aging* 5, no. 1 (1990): 41–47.

14. Atsuko Sugisawa, H. Sugisawa, Y. Nakatani, and H. Shibata, "Effect of Retirement on Mental Health and Social Well-being among Elderly Japanese," *Japanese Journal of Public Health* 44, no. 2 (1997): 123–30.

15. Marilyn K. Potts, "Social Support and Depression among Older Adults Living Alone: The Importance of Friends Within and Outside of a Retirement Community," *Social Work* 42, no. 4 (1997): 348–62.

16. Saraswati Mishra, "Leisure Activities and Life Satisfaction in Old Age: A Case Study of Retired Government Employees Living in Urban Areas,"*Activities, Adaptation, and Aging* 16, no. 4 (1992): 7–26.

17. Freedman, *Prime Time*, 20.

18. Bruce S. Rabin, *Stress, Immune Function, and Health: The Connection* (New York: Wiley-Liss & Sons, 1999).

19. Yukako Honma, Y. Naruse, and S. Kagamimori, "Physio-social Activities and Active Life Expectancy, Life Expectancy in Japanese Elderly," *Japanese Journal of Public Health* 46, no. 5 (1999): 380–90.

20. Leland P. Bradford, "Can You Survive Your Retirement?"*Harvard Business Review* (December 1979): 103–109.

21. Ward Casscells, C. H. Hennekens, D. Evans, B. Rosener, R. A. De Silva, B. Lown, J. E. Davies, and M. J. Jesse, "Retirement and Coronary Mortality," *The Lancet* (14 June 1980): 1288–89.

22. E. R. Gonzalez, "Retiring May Predispose to Fatal Heart Attack," *Journal of the American Medical Association* 243 (1980): 13–14.

23. B. Jonsson, I. Sernbo, H. Kristensson, and O. Johnell, "Hip Fractures in Middle-aged Men: A Consequence of Early Retirement and Alcohol Misuse?"*Alcohol & Alcoholism* 28, no. 6 (1993): 709–14.

24. Vilho Mattila, Matti Joukamaa, and Raimo Salokangas, "Retirement, Aging, Psychosocial Adaptation and Mortality: Some Findings of a Follow-up Study (The TURVA Project)," *European Journal of Psychiatry* 4, no. 3 (1990): 147–58.

25. James S. House, C. Robbins, and H. L. Metzner, "The Association of Social Relationships and Activities with Mortality: Prospective Evidence from the Tecumseh Community Health Study," *American Journal of Epidemiology* 116 (1982): 123–40.

26. John P. Robinson and Gordon Godby, *Time for Life: Surprising Ways that Americans Use Their Time* (University Park, Pa.: Pennsylvania State University Press, 1999), 136–54.

27. David J. Ekerdt, L. Baden, R. Bosse, and E. Dibbs, "The Effects of Retirement on Physical Health," *American Journal of Public Health* 73 (1983): 779–83.

28. Timo Niemi, "Retirement and Mortality," *Scandinavian Journal of Social Medicine* 8, no. 1 (1980): 39–41.

29. Timo Niemi, "The Mortality of Male Old-age Pensioners Following Spouse's Death," *Scandinavian Journal of Social Medicine* 7, no. 3 (1979): 115–17.

30. Tanya R. Fitzpatrick and R. Bosse, "Employment and Health among Older Bereaved Men in the Normative Aging Study: One Year and Three Years Following a Bereavement Event," *Social Work and Health Care* 32, no. 2 (2000): 41–60.

31. Jan E. Mutchler, J. A. Burr, M. P. Massagli, and A. Pienta, "Work Transitions and Health in Later Life," *Journal of Gerontology* 54, no. 5 (1999): 252–61.

32. Yael Benyamini, "The Bases for Predicting One's Mortality: The Relationship between the Predictors of Self-assessments of Health and the Predictors of Mortality," *Dissertation Abstracts International* 57, no. 11-B (May 1997): 7243.

33. Ming Wei, J. B. Kampert, C. E. Barlow, M. Z. Nichaman, L. W. Gibbons, R. S. Paffenbarger, Jr., and S. N. Blair, "Relationship between Low Cardiorespiratory Fitness and Mortality in Normal-weight, Overweight, and Obese Men," *Journal of the American Medical Association* 282, no. 16 (1999): 1547–53.

34. Mirja Hirvensalo, T. Rantanen, E. Heikkinen, "Mobility Difficulties and Physical Activity as Predictors of Mortality and Loss of Independence in the Community-living Older Population," *Journal of the American Geriatrics Society* 48, no. 5 (2000): 493-98.

35. Douglas Oman, C. E. Thoresen, and K. McMahon, "Volunteerism and Mortality among the Community-dwelling Elderly," *Journal of Health Psychology* 4 (1999): 301–16.

36. Douglas L. Lawson, *More Give to Live: How Giving Can Change Your Life* (San Diego: ALTI Publishing, 1999), 27–28.

37. David C. McClelland, "The Effect of Motivational Arousal through Films on Salivary Immunoglobulin A," *Psychology and Health* 2 (1988): 31–52.

CHAPTER 4: THE ALTERNATIVE

1. E. Payne, S. Robbins, and L. Dougherty, "Goal Directedness and Older-adult Adjustment," *Journal of Counseling Psychology* 38, no. 3 (1991): 302–308.

2. Victor Frankl, *Man's Search for Meaning* (New York: Pocket Books, 1959).

3. Erik Erikson, *Vital Involvement in Old Age: The Experience of Old Age in Our Time* (New York: Norton, 1994).

4. Christopher Ian Chenoweth, "Make a Small Difference in a Big Way," *Daily Inspiration* (29 November 2001); available from http://www.positivechristianity.org.

5. Harold G. Koenig, *Chronic Pain: Biomedical and Spiritual Approaches* (Binghamton, N.Y.: Haworth Press, 2002).

6. Jodie L. Waisberg and J. E. Porter, "Purpose in Life and Outcome of Treatment for Alcohol Dependence," *British Journal of Clinical Psychology* 33, no. 1 (1994): 49–63.

7. Stephanie Carroll, "Spirituality and Purpose in Life in Alcoholism Recovery," *Journal of Studies on Alcohol* 54, no 3 (1993): 297–301.

8. Lisa L. Harlow, M. D. Newcomb, and P. M. Bentler, "Depression, Self-derogation, Substance Use, and Suicide Ideation: Lack of Purpose in Life as a Mediational Factor," *Journal of Clinical Psychology* 42, no. 1 (1986): 5–21.

9. Sheryl Zika and Kerry Chamberlain, "On the Relation between Meaning in Life and Psychological Well-being," *British Journal of Psychology* 83, no. 1 (1992): 133–45.

10. Lawrence Weinstein, X. Xie, and C. C. Cleanthous, "Purpose in Life, Boredom, and Volunteerism in a Group of Retirees," *Psychological Reports* 76, no. 2 (1995): 482.

11. Herbert Rappaport, Robert J. Fossler, Laura S. Bross, and Dona Gilden, "Future Time, Death Anxiety, and Life Purpose among Older Adults," *Death Studies* 17, no. 4 (July-August 1993): 369–79.

12. Carol L. McWilliam, J. B. Brown, J. L. Carmichael, and J. M. Lehman, "A New Perspective on Threatened Autonomy in Elderly Persons: The Disempowering Process," *Social Science & Medicine* 38, no. 2 (1994): 327–38.

13. E. J. Taylor, "Factors Associated with Meaning in Life among People with Recurrent Cancer," *Oncology Nursing Forum* 20, no. 9 (1993): 1399–405.

14. Karen Hooker and Ilene C. Siegler, "Life Goals, Satisfaction, and Self-rated Health: Preliminary Findings," *Experimental Aging Research* 19 (1993): 97–110.

15. A. Grand, P. Gorsclaude, H. Bocquet, J. Pous, and J. L. Albarede, "Predictive Value of Life Events, Psychosocial Factors, and Self-rated Health on Disability in an Elderly Rural French Population," *Social Science and Medicine* 27 (1988): 1337–42.

16. George T. Reker, E. J. Peacock, and P. T. Wong, "Meaning and Purpose in Life and Well-being: A Life-span Perspective," *Journal of Gerontology* 42, no. 1 (1987): 44–9.

17. Yukako Honma, Y. Naruse, and S. Kagamimori, "Physio-social Activities and Active Life Expectancy, Life Expectancy in Japanese Elderly," *Japanese Journal of Public Health* 46, no. 5 (1999): 380–90.

18. Carolyn Milne, C. Saccco, G. Cetinski, G. Browne, and J. Roberts, "Correlates of Well-being among Caregivers of Cognitively Impaired Relatives," *Canadian Journal of Nursing Research* 26, no. 1 (1994): 27–39.

19. Kathleen M. Stetz, "The Relationship among Background Characteristics, Purpose in Life, and Caregiving Demands on Perceived Health of Spouse Caregivers," *Scholarly Inquiry for Nursing Practice* 3, no. 2 (1989): 133–53.

CHAPTER 5: VOLUNTEER

1. Robert Putnam, "Bowling Alone: America's Declining Social Capital," *Journal of Democracy* 6 (1995): 65–78.

2. Ibid., 67.

3. Bureau of the Census, *Projections of the Total Resident Population by 5-Year Age Groups, and Sex with Special Age Categories: Middle Series, 1999 to 2100;* available from: http://www.census.gov/population/projections/nation/summary/np-t3-f.pdf (Washington, D.C., 2001).

4. L. P. Fried, M. Freedman, T. E. Endres, and B. Wasik, "Building Communities That Promote Successful Aging," *Western Journal of Medicine* 167, no. 4 (1997): 216–19.

5. Marc Freedman, *Prime Time: How Baby Boomers Will Revolutionize Retirement and Transform America* (New York: Public Affairs Publishers, 1999), 17.

6. See http://www.census.gov/prod/2000pubs/p20-523.pdf.

7. Erik Erikson, *Vital Involvement in Old Age: The Experience of Old Age in Our Time* (New York: Norton, 1994).

8. James E. Curtis, E. Grabb, and D. Baer, "Voluntary Association Membership in 15 Countries: The Comparative Analysis,"*American Sociological Review* 57 (1992): 139–52.

9. *The New Non-Profit Almanac: Facts and Figures on the Independent Sector, 2001* (Washington, D.C.: The Independent Sector, 2001); available from http://www.indepsec.org/.

10. Ibid.

11. Freedman, *Prime Time*, 18.

12. Juliet B. Schor, *The Overworked American* (New York: Basic Books, 1991).

13. John Rowe and Robert L. Kahn, *Successful Aging* (New York: Pantheon Books, 1998).

14. *New Non-Profit Almanac 2001*.

15. Ibid.

16. D. H. Smith, "Determinants of Voluntary Association Participation and Volunteering: A Literature Review," *Nonprofit and Voluntary Sector Quarterly* 23 (1994): 243–63.

17. Howard V. Hayghe, "Volunteers in the United States: Who Donates the Time?" *Monthly Labor Review* 114 (1991): 17–23.

18. Lucy R. Fischer and Kay B. Schaffer, *Older Volunteers* (Thousand Oaks, Calif.: Sage Publications, 1993).

19. Virginia A. Hodgkinson and Robert Wuthnow, *Faith and Philanthropy in America* (San Francisco: Jossey-Bass, 1990).

20. Jerry Z. Park and C. Smith, "To whom much has been given ...: Religious Capital and Community Voluntarism among Churchgoing Protestants," *Journal for the Scientific Study of Religion* 39 (2000): 272–86.

21. John Wilson and Marc A. Musick, "Work and Volunteering: The Long Arm of the Job," *Social Forces* 76 (1997): 251–73.

22. Marc A. Musick, J. Wilson, and W. B. Bynum, "Race and Formal Volunteering: Differential Effects of Class and Religion," *Social Forces* 78 (2000): 1539–71.

23. J. L. Latting, "Motivational Differences between Black and White Volunteers," *Nonprofit and Voluntary Sector Quarterly* 19 (1990): 121–36.

24. Douglas L. Lawson, *More Give to Live: How Giving Can Change Your Life* (San Diego: ALTI Publishing, 1999), 18.

25. E. Gil Clary, M. Snyder, R. D. Ridge, J. Copeland, A. A. Stukas, J. Haugen, and P. Miene, "Understanding and Assessing the Motivations of Volunteers: A Functional Approach," *Journal of Personality and Social Psychology* 74 (1998): 1516–30.

26. Lawson, *More Give to Live*, 34–35.

27. George B. Stefano, G. L. Fricchione, B. T. Glingsby, and H. Benson, "The Placebo Effect and Relaxation Response: Neural Processes and Their Coupling to Constitutive Nitric Oxide," *Brain Research Reviews* 35 (2001): 1–19.

28. Lawson, *More Give to Live*, 34–35.

29. Ibid., 46.

30. Douglas Oman, C. E. Thoresen, and K. McMahon, "Volunteerism and Mortality among the Community-dwelling Elderly," *Journal of Health Psychology* 4 (1999): 301–16.

31. John R. Ellis, "Volunteerism as an Enhancement to Career Development," *Journal of Employment Counseling* 30, no. 3 (1993): 127–32.

32. Lynn I. Wasserbauer, D. T. Arrington, I. L. Abraham, "Using Elderly Volunteers to Care for the Elderly: Opportunities for Nursing," *Nursing Economics* 14 (1996): 232–38.

33. Gaye Heathcote, "Autonomy, Health and Aging: Transnational Perspectives," *Health Education Research* 15 (2000): 13–24.

34. Elizabeth Midlarsky and Eva Kahana, *Altruism in Later Life* (Thousand Oaks, Calif.: Sage Publications, 1994).

35. George Vaillant, *Adaptation to Life* (Boston: Little & Brown, 1977).

36. Neal Krause, A. R. Herzog, and E. Baker, "Providing Support to Others and Well-being in Later Life," *Journal of Gerontology* 47 (1992): 300–11.

37. Sula Benet, *Abkhasians: The Long-Living People of the Caucasus* (New York: Harcourt Brace College Publishers, 1974).

38. Oman et al., "Volunteerism."

39. Neal Krause, B. Ingersoll-Dayton, J. Liang, and H. Sugisawa. "Religion, Social Support, and Health among the Japanese Elderly," *Journal of Health & Social Behavior* 40 (1999): 405–21.

40. Robert N. Butler, *Why Survive? Growing Old in America* (New York: Harper & Row, 1975), 80–86.

41. Lawson, *More Give to Live.*

42. Marlene Wilson, *How to Mobilize Church Volunteers* (Minneapolis: Augsburg, 1983), 22–23.

43. Jenny Hainsworth and Julie Barlow, "Volunteers' Experiences of Becoming Arthritis Self-management Lay Leaders: 'It's almost as if I've stopped aging and started to get younger!'" *Arthritis & Rheumatism* 45, no. 4 (2001): 378–83.

CHAPTER 6: CULTIVATE GENEROSITY

1. See http://www.census.gov/prod/2001pubs/p60-213.pdf.

2. "In 'Over Our Heads': Credit Card Company Write-offs Set to Hit a Record High, an S&P Report Finds," in *CNN/Money*, 26 December 2001; available from http://money.cnn.com/2001/12/26/debt/q_credit/index.htm.

3. Angela Swanson, "St. Christopher's Hospice awarded $1 million: London Hospice gets Hilton Humanitarian Prize," *Research News & Opportunities in Science and Theology* 2(3) (2001): 26.

4. Albert J. Edmonds, *Buddhist and Christian Gospels: Now First Compared from the Originals: "Gospel Parallels from Pali Texts,"* ed. Masaharu Anesaki, 4th ed., 2 vols. (Philadelphia: Innes & Sons, 1914), 22.

5. Christopher Ian Chenoweth, *Daily Inspiration* (3 December 2001); available from http://www.PositiveChristianity.org

6. Refers to net official development assistance (ODA) given by developed nations to developing countries and multilateral organizations. ODA is financial assistance that is concessional, has as its main objective promotion of the economic development and welfare of the less developed countries, and contains a grant element of at least 25 percent. The entry does not include other official flows or private flows. Data are for 1995–98.

7. *The World Factbook 2000*; available from http://www.odci.gov/cia/publications/factbook/indexgeo.html.

8. *The New Non-Profit Almanac: Facts and Figures on the Independent Sector, 2001* (Washington, D.C.: The Independent Sector, 2001); available from http://www.indepsec.org/.

9. Douglas L. Lawson, *More Give to Live: How Giving Can Change Your Life* (San Diego: ALTI Publishing, 1999), 13–14.

10. *New Non-Profit Almanac 2001*.

11. Lawson, *More Give to Live*, 14.

12. *New Non-Profit Almanac 2001*.

13. Lawson, *More Give to Live*, 116.

14. Harold G. Koenig, Kenneth I. Pargament, and J. Nielsen, "Religious Coping and Health Outcomes in Medically Ill Hospitalized Older Adults," *Journal of Nervous & Mental Disorders* 186 (1998): 513–21.

CHAPTER 7: DEVELOP SPIRITUALLY

1. Sigmund Freud, *Civilization and Its Discontents, Standard Edition of the Complete Psychological Works of Sigmund Freud*, ed. and trans. James Strachey (1930; repr. London: Hogarth Press, 1962), 25.

2. Os Guinness, *Long Journey Home: A Guide to Your Search for the Meaning of Life* (New York: Doubleday, 2001).

3. Harold G. Koenig, "An 83-year-old Woman with Chronic Illness and Strong Religious Beliefs," *Journal of the American Medical Association* (in press).

4. Mark A. Schuster, B. D. Stein, L. H. Jaycox, R. L. Collins, G. N. Marshall, M. N. Elliott, A. J. Zhou, D. E. Kanouse, J. L. Morrison, and S. H. Berry, "A National Survey of Stress Reactions after the September 11, 2001, Terrorist Attacks," *New England Journal of Medicine* 345 (2001): 1507–12.

5. Harold G. Koenig, Michael E. McCullough, and David B. Larson, *Handbook of Religion and Health* (New York: Oxford University Press, 2001).

6. Harold G. Koenig, *The Healing Connection* (Nashville: Word, 2001).

7. Paul Mueller, D. J. Plevak, T. A. Rummans, "Religious Involvement, Spirituality, and Medicine: Subject Review and Implications for Clinical Practice," *Mayo Clinic Proceedings* 76 (2001): 1225–36.

8. Harold G. Koenig and H. J. Cohen, *The Link Between Religion and Health: Psychoneuroimmunology and the Faith Factor* (New York: Oxford University Press, 2002).

9. Koenig et al., *Handbook of Religion and Health*.

10. *The Living Bible* (Wheaton, Ill.: Tyndale House, 1971).

11. David B. Winter, *Closer Than a Brother: Practicing the Presence of God* (Wheaton, Ill.: Harold Shaw Publishers, 1971).

12. Thomas à Kempis, *The Imitation of Christ*, 1617 (New York: Random House, 1998).

13. Mother Teresa and Jaya Chaliha, *The Joy in Loving*, ed. Edward Le Joly (New York: Penguin/Viking, 2000).

14. John Bunyan, *The Pilgrim's Progress*, 1678 (Nashville: Thomas Nelson, 1999).

15. C. S. Lewis, *Mere Christianity*, 1943 (San Francisco: Harper, 2001).

16. Charles M. Sheldon, *In His Steps* (Fort Worth, Tex.: Brownlow, 1982).

17. Hannah Hurnard, *Hinds' Feet on High Places* (Wheaton, Ill.: Tyndale, 1975).

18. Bruce Wilkinson, *The Prayer of Jabez* (Sisters, Ore.: Multnomah, 2000).

19. Edith Schaeffer, *Affliction: A Compassionate Look at the Reality of Pain and Suffering* (Grand Rapids, Mich.: Baker, 1978).

20. Rabbi Sidney Schwarz, *Finding a Spiritual Home: How a New Generation of Jews Can Transform the American Synagogue* (San Francisco: Jossey-Bass, 2000).

21. David Aaron, *Endless Light: The Ancient Path of the Kabbalah to Love, Spiritual Growth, and Personal Power* (New York: Penguin-Putnam, 1998).

22. Barry W. Holtz, *Back to the Sources: Reading the Classic Jewish Texts* (New York: Simon & Schuster, 1986).

23. N. J. Dawood, *The Koran* (New York: Penguin, 1990).

24. Maulana Muhammad Ali, *The Holy Quran: Arabic Text, English Translation and Commentary Revised Edition* (Lahore, Pakistan: Ahmadiyya Anjuman Ishaat Islam Lahore, Inc., 1983).

25. Daniel J. Ladinsky, trans., *Gift: Poems by Hafiz the Great Sufi Master* (New York: Penguin Putman, 1999).

26. Guinness, *Long Journey Home*; and Os Guinness, *The Call* (Nashville: Word, 1998).

27. Karen Armstrong, *A History of God: The 4000-Year Quest for Judaism, Christianity and Islam* (New York: Random House, 1994).

28. Herbert Benson, *The Relaxation Response* (New York: William Morrow, 1975); and Herbert Benson, *Timeless Healing* (New York: Simon & Schuster, 1997).

29. Dalai Lama, *An Open Heart: Practicing Compassion in Everyday Life*, ed. N. Vreeland (New York: Little, Brown & Company, 2001); and Dalai Lama and H. C. Cutler, *The Art of Happiness: A Handbook for Living* (New York: Putnam, 1998).

CHAPTER 8: REDUCE STRESS

1. Walter B. Cannon, "The Emergency Function of the Adrenal Medulla in Pain and the Major Emotions," *American Journal of Physiology* 33 (1941): 356.

2. Bruce S. Rabin, *Stress, Immune Function, and Health: The Connection* (New York: Wiley-Liss & Sons, 1999).

3. L. E. Hinkle, "Stress and Disease: The Concept after 50 Years," *Social Science & Medicine* 25, no. 6 (1987): 561–66.

4. Ronald B. Herberman, "Principles of Tumor Immunology," *Textbook of Clinical Oncology*, ed. AI Holleb, D. J. Fink, and G. P. Murphy (Atlanta: American Cancer Society, 1991), 69–79.

5. Sandra Levy, M. Lippman, and T. d'Angelo, "Correlation of Stress Factors with Sustained Suppression of Natural Killer Cell Activity and Predictive Prognosis in Patients with Breast Cancer," *Journal of Clinical Oncology* 5 (1987): 348–53.

6. Sandra Levy, J. Lee, C. Bagley, and G. Lippman, "Survival Hazards Analysis in First Recurrent Breast Cancer Patients: The Seven-year Follow-up," *Psychosomatic Medicine*, 50 (1988): 520–28.

7. D. Roberts, B. L. Andersen, and D. Lubaroff, "Stress and Immunity at Cancer Diagnosis," Department of Psychology, Ohio State University, Columbus, Ohio, 1994.

8. Ronald Glaser, B. Rabin, M. Chesney, S. Cohen, and B. Natelson, "Stress-induced Immunomodulation: Implications for Infectious Diseases?" *Journal of the American Medical Association* 281, no. 24 (1999): 2268–70.

9. Gail Ironson, A. LaPerrier, M. Antoni, P. O'Hearn, N. Schneiderman, N. Klimas, and M. A. Fletcher, "Changes in Immune and Psychological Measures as a Function of Anticipation and Reaction to News of HIV-A Antibody Status," *Psychosomatic Medicine* 52 (1990): 247–70.

10. Dwight L. Evans, J. Leserman, D. O. Perkins, R. A. Stern, C. Murphy, B. Zheng, D. Gettes, J. A. Longmate, S. G. Silva, C. M. van der Horst, C. D. Hall, J. D. Folds, R. N. Golden, and J. M Petitto, "Severe Life Stress as a Predictor of Early Disease Progression in HIV Infection," *American Journal of Psychiatry* 154 (1997): 630–34.

11. Janice Kiecolt-Glaser, J. R. Dura, C. E. Speicher, O. J. Trask, and R. Glaser, "Spousal Caregivers of Dementia Victims: Longitudinal Changes in Immunity and Health," *Psychosomatic Medicine* 53 (1991): 345–62.

12. Janice Kiecolt-Glaser, R. Glaser, S. Gravenstein, W. B. Malarkey, and J. Sheridan, "Chronic Stress Alters the Immune Response to Influenza

Virus Vaccine in Older Adults," *Proceedings of the National Academy of Sciences of the United States of America* 93 (1996): 3043–47.

13. Janice Kiecolt-Glaser, W. Garner, and C. Spelcher, "Psychosocial Modifiers of Immunocompetence in Medical Students," *Psychosomatic Medicine* 46 (1984): 7–14.

14. Sheldon Cohen, D. A. J. Tyrell, and A. P. Smith, "Psychological Stress and Susceptibility to the Common Cold," *New England Journal of Medicine* 325 (1991): 606–12.

15. Anika Rosengren, G. Tibblin, and L. Wilhelmsen, "Self-perceived Psychological Stress and Incidence of Coronary Artery Disease in Middle-aged Men," *American Journal of Cardiology* 68 (1991): 1171–75.

16. Dominique L. Musselman, D. L. Evans, and C. B. Nemeroff, "The Relationship of Depression to Cardiovascular Disease: Epidemiology, Biology, and Treatment," *Archives of General Psychiatry* 55 (1998): 580–92.

17. Alexander H. Glassman and P. A. Shapiro, "Depression and the Course of Coronary Artery Disease," *American Journal of Psychiatry* 155 (1998): 4–11.

18. Redford Williams and V. Williams, *Anger Kills* (New York: HarperCollins, 1998).

19. Sharon L. Larson, P. L. Owens, D. Ford, and W. Eaton, "Depressive Disorder, Dysthymia, and Risk of Stroke: Thirteen-year Follow-up from the Baltimore Epidemiologic Catchment Area Study," *Stroke* 32, no. 9 (2001): 1979–83.

20. Janice Kiecolt-Glaser, P. T. Marucha, W. B. Malarkey, A. M. Mercado, and R. Glaser, "Slowing of Wound Healing by Psychological Stress," *Lancet* 346, no. 8984 (1996): 1194–96.

21. Phillip T. Marucha, Janice Kiecolt-Glaser, and M. Favagehi, "Mucosal Wound Healing Is Impaired by Examinations Stress," *Psychosomatic Medicine* 60 (1998): 362–65.

22. Bert N. Uchino, J. R. Cacioppo, and Janice Kiecolt-Glaser, "The Relationship between Social Support and Physiological Processes: A Review with Emphasis on Underlying Mechanisms and Implications for Health," *Psychological Bulletin* 119 (1996): 488–531.

23. Robert M. Sapolsky, S. C. Alberts, and J. Altman, "Hypercortisolism Associated with Social Subordinance or Social Isolation among Wild Baboons," *Archives of General Psychiatry* 54 (1997): 1137–43.

24. Janice Kiecolt-Glaser, D. Ricker, J. George, "Urinary Cortisol Levels, Cellular Immunocompetence, and Loneliness in Psychiatric Inpatients," *Psychosomatic Medicine* 46 (1984): 15–23.

25. Kiecolt-Glaser et al., "Psychosocial Modifiers."

26. Kiecolt-Glaser et al., "Spousal Caregivers."

27. Robert S. Baron, C. E. Cutrona, D. Hicklin, D. W. Russel, and D. M. Lubaroff, "Social Support and Immune Function among Spouses of Cancer Patients," *Journal of Personality and Social Psychology* 59 (1990): 344–52.

28. Levy et al., "Correlation of Stress Factors."

29. Sandra Levy, R. B. Herberman, J. Lee, I. Whiteside, J. Kirkwood, and S. McFeeley, "Estrogen Receptor Concentration and Social Factors as Predictors of Natural Killer Cell Activity in Early-stage Breast Cancer Patients," *Natural Immunity and Cell Growth Regulation* 9 (1990): 313–24.

30. David Spiegel, J. R. Bloom, H. C. Kraemer, and E. Gottheil, "Effect of Psychosocial Treatment on Survival of Patients with Metastatic Breast Cancer," *Lancet* 2, no. 8668 (1989): 888–91.

31. David Spiegel, "A 43-year-old Woman Coping with Cancer," *Journal of the American Medical Association* 282 (1999): 371–78.

32. Daren C. Greenwood, K. R. Muir, C. J. Packham, and R. J. Madley, "Coronary Heart Disease: A Review of the Role of Psychosocial Stress and Social Support," *Journal of Public Health Medicine* 18 (1996): 221–31.

33. Teresa Seeman and S. L. Syme, "Social Networks and Coronary Artery Disease: A Comparison of the Structure and Function of Social Relations as Predictors of Disease," *Psychosomatic Medicine* 49 (1987): 341–54.

34. Redford B. Williams, J. C. Barefoot, R. M. Califf, T. L. Haney, W. B. Saunders, D. B. Pryor, M. A. Hlatky, I. C. Siegler, and D. B. Mark, "Prognostic Importance of Social and Economic Resources among Medically Treated Patients with Angiographically Documented Coronary Artery Disease," *Journal of the American Medical Association* 267 (1992): 520–24.

35. David Burns, *Feeling Good: The New Mood Therapy* (New York: William Morrow, 1999).

36. M. Basil Pennington, *Centering Prayer: Renewing an Ancient Christian Prayer Form* (New York: Doubleday, 1980).

37. Jon Kabat-Zinn, A. O. Massion, J. Kristeller, L. G. Peterson, K. E. Fletcher, L. Pbert, W. R. Lenderking, and S. F. Santorelli, "Effectiveness of a Meditation-based Stress Reduction Program in the Treatment of Anxiety Disorders," *American Journal of Psychiatry* 149 (1992): 936–43.

38. Jon Kabat-Zinn, L. Lipworth, and R. Burney, "The Clinical Use of Mindfulness Meditation for the Self-regulation of Chronic Pain," *Journal of Behavioral Medicine* 8 (1985): 163–90.

Chapter 9: Live Healthy

1. Nanci Hellmich, "61% of Americans Overweight, Latest Health Survey Finds," *USA Today*, (December 15, 2000).

2. Food and Drug Administration, Center for Food Safety and Applied Nutrition, Department of Health and Human Services, *Nutrition and Your Health: Dietary Guidelines for Americans*, 4th ed., USDA report, 1995.

3. Andrew Stoll, *The Omega-3 Connection* (New York: Simon & Schuster, 2001).

4. L. A. Kamimoto, A. N. Easton, E. Maurice, C. G. Husten, and C. A. Macera, "Surveillance for Five Health Risks Among Older Adults—United States, 1993–1997," *Mortality and Morbidity Weekly Reports* 48, ss. 08 (1999): 89–130.

5. Available from http://www.weightchart.org.

6. Anita L. Stewart, C. J. Verboncoeur, B. Y. McLellan, D. E. Gillis, S. Rush, K. M. Mills, A. C. King, P. Ritter, B. W. Brown, and W. M. Bortz, "Physical Activity Outcomes of CHAMPS II: A Physical Activity Promotion Program for Older Adults," *Journals of Gerontology* 56, no. 8 (2001): M465–70.

7. Hussain R. Yusuf, J. B. Croft, and W. H. Giles, "Leisure-time Physical Activity among Older Adults, United States, 1990," *Archives of Internal Medicine* 156 (1996): 1321–26.

8. B. J. George and N. Goldberg, "The Benefits of Exercise in Geriatric Women," *American Journal of Geriatric Cardiology* 10, no. 5 (2001): 260–63.

9. Martha L. Slattery and David R. Jacobs, Jr., "Physical Fitness and Cardiovascular Disease Mortality: The U.S. Railroad Study," *American Journal of Epidemiology* 127, no. 3 (1988): 571–80.

10. Christer Janson, E. Lindberg, T. Gislason, A. Elmasry, and G. Boman, "Insomnia in Men: A 10-year Prospective Population Based Study," *Sleep* 24, no. 4 (2001): 425–30.

11. Nina Haapanen-Niemi, S. Miilunpalo, M. Pasanen, I. Vuori, P. Oja, and J. Malmberg, "Body Mass Index, Physical Inactivity and Low Level of Physical Fitness as Determinants of All-Cause and Cardiovascular Disease Mortality: 16-year Follow-up of Middle-aged and Elderly Men and Women," *International Journal of Obesity* 24, no. 11 (2000): 1465–74.

12. Stewart et al., "Physical Activity Outcomes."

13. Carl J. Caspersen, G. M. Christenson, and R. A. Pollard, "Status of the 1990 Physical Fitness and Exercise Objectives: Evidence from NHIS-1985," *Public Health Reports* 101 (1986): 587–92.

14. Janet H. McHenry, *PrayerWalk* (Colorado Springs, Colo.: WaterBrook Press, 2001).

15. Ibid.

16. "Cigarette Smoking among Adults: United States, 1994," *Mortality and Morbidity Weekly Reports* 45 (1996): 588–90.

17. Jodie L. Waisberg and James E. Porter, "Purpose in Life and Outcome of Treatment for Alcohol Dependence," *British Journal of Clinical Psychology* 33 (1994): 49–63.

CONCLUSION

1. Krishna quotation from Sanderson Beck's translation; available from http://www.san.beck.org/Gita.html.

2. Lionel Giles, ed., *The Sayings of Confucius* (Boston: Charles E. Tuttle, 1993).

❧ Index

Tables are indicated by a "t" following the page reference